Joseph Conrad Today

Kieron O'Hara

SOCIETAS
essays in political
& cultural criticism

imprint-academic.com

Published in the UK by Societas
Imprint Academic, PO Box 200, Exeter EX5 5YX, UK

Published in the USA by Societas
Imprint Academic, Philosophy Documentation Center
PO Box 7147, Charlottesville, VA 22906-7147, USA

ISBN 9781845400668

A CIP catalogue record for this book is available from the
British Library and US Library of Congress

Contents

For Professor Rebecca Hughes

Chapter One

Still Sprightly at 150

It has been written that Joseph Conrad, great novelist of English, aristocratic stylist, pioneer of modernism, led three lives.[1] He was the child of romantic Polish revolutionaries, from Berdyczów, a small town perpetually caught up in Great Power tugs of war, Lithuanian and Polish territory until the Second Partition of Poland in 1793 when it was annexed to Russia; it is now part of the Ukraine. Józef Teodor Konrad Nalecz Korzeniowski was born a Pole, a nationality that no longer existed, on 3rd December 1857. At the age of 17, he began a second life as a seaman, based originally in Marseilles, then England. And at the age of 31, he began writing a story that evolved into his first novel, *Almayer's Folly*. It is this third life as a literary giant, author of fourteen novels, seven collections of stories, four collections of essays, plus a few plays and minor collaborations, that ensures Conrad's lasting fame.

Conrad's last novel, *The Rover*, was published in December 1923, and the bulk of his best work completed prior to the commencement of hostilities in 1914. In many ways, his world was unbelievably remote from ours. The 20th century has given us extraordinary technological progress, undreamt-of prosperity, a spread of education and culture. Religion has waned and ideology waxed, superpowers risen and fallen, all against the background of fiercely murderous conflict across the globe.

Yet what strikes the reader of Conrad's great works, *Nostromo*, *The Secret Agent*, 'Heart of darkness', is their extraordinary *relevance* to the politics of our age. More than, say, Orwell's *Nineteen Eighty-Four* or Koestler's *Darkness at Noon*, to choose two magnificent political novels of the 20th century, Conrad speaks to us directly. He communicates at a human level; he is close to Tolstoy in his ability to connect the individual with the global, the contingent human decision with

---

[1]   Frederick R. Karl, *Joseph Conrad: The Three Lives*, London: Faber and Faber, 1979.

the overarching political implications. Despite the technologically-inspired erosion of privacy of our era,[2] *Nineteen Eighty-Four* still reads like a nightmare, a science fiction dystopia. Though it may be a possible end point of current trends, it is not here and now. But the author of *Nostromo* might easily be commenting directly on events in Venezuela or Bolivia in 2007; *The Secret Agent* might have been inspired by the attacks on the London Underground network in July 2005, instead of that on the Greenwich Observatory in 1894. 'Heart of darkness' might have been set in Iraq.

In this book, my aim is to expand on the idea that an old-fashioned, crotchety, highly-strung novelist, living in relatively straitened circumstances as an exile writing in a foreign language, who (according to the self-consciously modern H.G. Wells) was not serious about social and political issues, had no sense of humour and a "ridiculous" persona "of a romantic adventurous un-mercenary intensely artistic European gentleman carrying an exquisite code of unblemished honour through a universe of baseness"[3] — nevertheless speaks loudly and accurately in the world of George W. Bush, Osama bin-Laden, the World Wide Web, neo-liberalism and anti-globalisation. Is it his political wisdom? His understanding of the human condition? His experience of life?

And can his vision, pessimistic, self-consciously marginal and at times bordering on the nihilistic, inform us about the choices ahead of us? Can imaginative writings, one hundred years old, really be more *au point* than those of today's learned commentariat? Particularly as Conrad now has to be seen through the haze of a century of critical analysis. He has been adulated, despite manifest failings in even his greatest books. He has been called a racist, a sexist and an imperialist. One recent project was even dedicated to:

> … the recovery, mapping, and invention of Conrad as a woman's writer, a lesbian writer, an African, Indian, Indonesian, Jewish, Palestinian, Native American, and U.S. writer, a hybrid writer (culturally or narratively), a "terrorist" writer, a working-class writer, an AIDS or a disabled writer, an older writer, an immigrant writer, a popular writer, a writer written out of the power

[2]   Kieron O'Hara & Nigel Shadbolt, *The Spy in the Coffee Machine*, Oxford: Oneworld, forthcoming.

[3]   Quoted in Jocelyn Baines, *Joseph Conrad: A Critical Biography*, Harmondsworth: Pelican, 1971, 285.

structure or beyond revolution by media and politics ... the secret Conrad of the twenty-first century.[4]

It is reasonably safe to say that Conrad would have been astounded with many of these reinventions, with the possibly exception, given his perpetual impecuniousness, of popularity.

He was obviously a man of great, if uneven, talent. It is rare to find such a person with little useful to say, and Conrad has plenty to say. But he was awkward and negative. Whatever one's theory, whatever one's positive vision, one will find oneself under retrospective attack from Conrad. That is hard to take for those who prefer their perspectives sharp, their paths clear, be they readers of Marx, Hayek, Chomsky, Billy Graham or L. Ron Hubbard.

But the world has six billion inhabitants, believing five billion different things. Some people take a year to earn $300, while others manage it every couple of minutes. Gods and creeds struggle for recognition in people's hearts and on their television screens. A few people are changing the very climate for everyone else. A few others threaten perpetual violence. Some wish to change their societies, others work hard to climb to the top of theirs. Still others wish merely to get by. In all this jumble, what path could be clear? What perspective could take in the whole scene?

Conrad is the stately chronicler of the human cacophony. His carefully crafted, slow, complex narratives relate the large to the small, individual decisions to the macro-level effects. Nothing in a Conradian world goes right, and nothing is what it seems. In one sense perspective is the last thing one would expect in his work — one of the very few metaphysical constants throughout his fiction is a brooding, inchoate darkness.

Novels, and art generally, are kinder to politics than is often thought. Writers often flatter themselves that they are exposing shams and evasions. Everyone looks down on the despised species of politicians, while few seem to worry overmuch about the evasions and shams of writers. But the often unstated assumption of an artistic commentator is that *alternatives exist*. The world may be run by businessmen, or the military-industrial complex, or the United States, or white people, and run badly (these propositions are of course true), but if only they could be resisted or deposed, all could

---

[4]   Carola Kaplan, Peter Lancelot Mallios & Andrea White, 'Introduction', in Carola M. Kaplan, Peter Lancelot Mallios & Andrea White (eds.), *Conrad in the Twenty-First Century: Contemporary Approaches and Perspectives*, New York: Routledge, 2005, xiii-xxii, at xix.

be well (that proposition may well be false, and the few revolution-ary occasions when it has been tested have not been happy ones). We can all agree that George Bush has made a mess of everything. But it does not follow from that evident truth that Hugo Chávez or Subcomandante Marcos would make a better job of it, even though they are cheered from the rafters from the safety of London or Paris for cocking a snook at everything Bush stands for. Conrad was not prey to that delusion, and exposes it time and again. That is what makes him awkward, and critics uncomfortable.

Korzeniowski[5]

Young Korzeniowski's origins were decidedly unusual. His father Apollo was a tortured soul, haunted by Poland's fate. Rather than hand out cigars upon the birth of young Józef, he penned a Christen-ing poem with the decidedly un-snappy title 'To my son born in the 85th year of Muscovite Oppression', including the cheery lines "You are without land, without love, without country, without people, while Poland — your mother — is in her grave."

The Korzeniowskis were a noble family whose extensive lands had been confiscated after a failed rebellion against Russian over-lords in 1830. In 1856, Apollo married Ewalina Bobrowska, from an equally aristocratic though somewhat less romantic family which, thanks to more judicious behaviour, had managed to keep some of its lands and fortune. The Bobrowskis, though patriotic Poles, were suspicious of what they considered the political extremism of the Korzeniowskis in general and Apollo in particular. With some rea-son.

He worked his way through his own money and his wife's dowry in a few years, and gave up his job to join the Polish revolutionary movement as an intellectual and poet, moving to Warsaw in 1861 as a leader of the radical patriots. Arrest was inevitable, and he spent seven months in prison, leaving Ewalina distraught and ill with the first signs of tuberculosis. Apollo's release was followed by exile to Vologda, some 500 gruelling kilometres North of Moscow; Ewalina and Conrad both nearly died of fever and illness on the journey. Conditions there were grim, Spartan and cold, although the authori-ties relented and allowed the Korzeniowskis to move further South after a year or so. Nevertheless, Ewalina died in 1865. Apollo sank into a profound spiritual melancholy: "I see what Dante did *not*

[5]   For information on Conrad's life, see the references given in 'Reading Conrad', at the end of this book.

describe, for his soul, appalled though it was with terror, was too Christian to harbour inhuman visions."[6] The weight on poor Conrad's shoulders must have been heavy; for his part, Apollo gave his son a quirky but rigorous education, and Conrad became a keen reader and French speaker. Their conditions of exile were relaxed still further, but Apollo's own health declined, and he died in Cracow in 1869.

The young orphan now became the ward of his mother's brother, Tadeusz Bobrowski, a pragmatic, generous, sensitive but realistic man who padded out Conrad's romanticism and aristocratic melancholy with a bit of common sense. Their funny relationship is mapped, in a one-sided way, by Tadeusz's letters to Conrad — often cross and frustrated by Conrad's fecklessness (a Korzeniowski trait, according to Tadeusz), but always loving and ultimately supportive. Conrad's letters back did not survive the Russian revolution.

Conrad's health remained delicate, necessitating private tutoring, but he still undertook a long European tour with an English companion in 1873, during which he saw salt water for the first time (in Venice), and began to formulate his ambition to go to sea. Poor Tadeusz initially reacted with horror, but Conrad was liable, as a Russian subject and convict's son, to 25 years' military service. Compared to that a seaman's career was infinitely more palatable. The physical exercise and clean air might also help Conrad's health.

Tadeusz financed Conrad's trip to the seaport of Marseilles in 1874, where he encountered colourful characters such as the shipowner M. Delastang (with whom he fell out — Conrad was a great faller-outer) who gave him his first sea-bound experiences, and Dominic Cervoni, (later immortalised as Nostromo, and as Dominic in *The Arrow of Gold*), the first mate of the *Sainte-Antoine* who may have taken Conrad on gun-running or smuggling expeditions. His first paid sea voyage was as an apprentice on the *Mont Blanc* sailing to the West Indies in 1875. But there was not enough work to support his lifestyle, and he quickly ran through Uncle Tadeusz's allowance; depressed and lonely, and without steady work, he borrowed money and lost it gambling. In 1878 he turned a gun to his chest and fired.

The bullet was close enough to his heart for us to believe it was a genuine suicide attempt, although he had also ensured that a friend was expected to tea shortly afterwards to discover and save him. The

---

[6]   From a letter of Apollo Korzeniowski's, of January 1866, quoted in Baines, *Joseph Conrad*, 35.

wound was passed off, characteristically romantically, as the result of a duel. Tadeusz, who had spent much of the intervening period writing Conrad scolding letters, rushed to Marseilles and put the lad back on his feet again. Together they worked out a plan to improve Conrad's prospects. There were administrative difficulties to advancement in French shipping, but the British mercantile marine was more accommodating to foreigners. Hence, later that year, Conrad joined a British ship, the *Mavis*, arriving at Lowestoft in June. After a small hiccup (the young man made straight for London and lost all his money again), he got himself a job on the *Skimmer of the Seas*, hauling coal between Lowestoft and Newcastle, before landing his biggest journey yet, on the *Duke of Sutherland* bound for Sydney. The most important part of that trip was upon the return in 1879, when Conrad sailed up the Thames, providing the seed for the striking imagery of darkness and impenetrability in 'Heart of darkness'. In 1880, to his uncle's absolute delight, he qualified as a second mate; in 1884, he passed his first mate's examination, and in 1886 he received his master's certificate. Some of his voyages were fictionalised more or less lightly in his later work.

Living on British ships, with international crews, perpetually travelling, permanently exiled, meant that Conrad was always wrestling with questions of identity, writing to a Polish friend that "in a free and hospitable land even the most persecuted of our race may find relative peace and a certain amount of happiness — materially at least … . When speaking, writing or thinking in English [as Conrad was in this letter, one of his first in English, in October 1885] the word Home always means for me the hospitable shores of Great Britain."[7] What a transformation this was; in one of his earliest surviving writings, carefully copied onto the back of a photograph sent to his grandmother, the 5-year-old Conrad signed himself "grandson, Pole, Catholic, nobleman—6 July 1863—Konrad." He transformed himself from the foreigner Korzeniowski to the more English sounding Conrad round about the middle of the 1880s. He stayed in epistolary touch with Tadeusz Bobrowski, meeting him in Marienbad in 1883, on his first return to Poland in 1890 some years after naturalising his British status, and again in 1893. A distant cousin living in Brussels, Marguerite Poradowska, a glamorous and beautiful novelist, was also an important influence. There is no

---

[7]   Conrad's letters, of which a number are quoted in this book, are available in
      a multi-volume edition, Frederick R. Karl & Laurence Davies (eds.), *The
      Collected Letters of Joseph Conrad*, Cambridge: Cambridge University Press.

doubt that Marguerite, whom Conrad always referred to as his 'Aunt', helped foster his growing literary ambitions. It is generally thought that his story 'The black mate', first published in 1908, was originally written for a competition in *Tit-Bits* magazine, of all places, in about 1886; if so it would be Conrad's earliest known literary work.

In 1890 he accepted a three-year appointment for the Société Anonyme Belge pour le Commerce du Haut-Congo, ostensibly to command a paddle-steamer sailing the 1,000 miles of the Congo River between Stanley Pool and Stanleyville. In the event, the steamer was damaged, and he never took command. After six months in the tropical climate, he was so ill his contract was terminated and he was shipped back to Europe, but not before he had witnessed appalling abuses, including the kidnapping and holding hostage of natives' families, forced labour, mutilations and the massive exploitation of Congolese ivory and rubber. As the supposed point of the so-called Congo Free State, privately owned by the King of the Belgians, Leopold II, one of the most evil men of the colonial period, was to bring civilisation to the Dark Continent and end the Arabic slave trade, this was hypocrisy on a grand scale.

Conrad's health had been poor since his forced exile as a child. He had needed treatment on an injured back in Singapore in 1887, and the Congo trip left him with malaria, dysentery, rheumatism and neuralgia. He would often, from 1890 onwards, decamp for weeks at a time to Swiss sanatoria. The outdoor, physical life was losing its lustre.

Conrad

It was during a long shore leave in Pimlico, in the Autumn of 1889, that Conrad began work on his first novel, and he carried the manuscript round the world with him for years, adding to it "line by line, not page by page".[8] As first mate on the *Torrens* on the way to Adelaide in 1892, he got his first reader, a passenger called W.H. Jacques who declared that *Almayer's Folly* was distinctly worth finishing. Ironically, Jacques died in 1893, only two months after arriving back in England.

With encouragement from his first English literary friend, future Nobel Prizewinner John Galsworthy, Marguerite Poradowska and others, Conrad finished the book in April 1894, a few weeks after the

---

[8]   From *A Personal Record.*

death of Tadeusz. Another influential friend was soon made. One of the readers of the manuscript employed by the publisher Fisher Unwin was Edward Garnett, who spotted Conrad's talent and recommended publication; he became a lifelong friend. *Almayer's Folly* was published in London in 1895, followed the next year by his second novel *An Outcast of the Islands*.

These two works were deep, self-consciously 'literary', slow and stately, and dealt with the same subject matter, the tangled relationships between different generations, sexes and races in the outposts of the Dutch empire in Borneo. They, and a third planned novel, *The Rescue* (finished only in 1920) used the same characters, and together made up a trilogy spanning thirty years of action between about 1860 and 1890 in reverse order: the events in *The Rescue* occur first, those of *Almayer's Folly* last. Conrad's ironic technique, scepticism and depressing outlook were already in place. His English style contained a few odd French and Polish constructions, but both early books are extremely well-written — incredible when one realises that English was his *third* language, and his spoken English remained heavily accented and hard to understand. Conrad had gone from being a sailor to a writer; in fact, he had transmuted almost directly from an unmarried sailor to a married writer, after courting a typist, Jessie George, some 16 years younger than him.

They were married in 1896, a few days after the publication of *An Outcast*, and set up home in Essex, where he made more literary contacts, H.G. Wells, Henry James, Stephen Crane and R.B. Cunninghame Graham — this latter a minor figure but a great friend to Conrad, receiver of some of his most profound letters and an inspiration for the plot of *Nostromo*. He also began writing short stories; Conrad was an extremely able writer of short fiction, although his ambitions were focused rather more on the fees than literary merit. 1898 saw the birth, to Conrad's mild horror, of a son, Borys. Another important acquaintance, of novelist Ford Madox Ford, was made later that year; Conrad and Ford would collaborate here and there over the next few years.

His third published novel, of 1897, was *The Nigger of the "Narcissus"*, in which he wrote for the first time about life on board ship. His understanding of a working life, and the peculiar relationships that bind a crew together, drives on the odd story about two workshy individuals who between them try to undermine the ship's corporate ethos. 1899 saw his most famous work, 'Heart of Darkness', based on his trip to the Congo, telling the tale of the last days of

Kurtz, a megalomaniacal ivory trader whose dreams of bringing civilisation to the African natives end in murder, exploitation and corruption. *Lord Jim* (1900) tells the story of a privileged young man torn apart by guilt after an act of cowardice.

None of these great works were getting Conrad much money, and he was also suffering increasingly frequently from gout and nervous depression. Furthermore, Jessie Conrad injured both legs in a fall about this time, which disabled her permanently and required several operations over the years. Nevertheless in 1904 he completed his most ambitious work, *Nostromo*, a story of revolution, greed, exploitation and power in a fictional South American republic; this is generally recognised as one of the key early modernist works in English literature. Several significant short stories also appeared, but his financial straits were strained further when his second son John was born in 1906.

The Secret Agent, a tale of seedy anarchists in a shabby London, was published in 1907, and his literary reputation was growing all the time. But matters were reaching a crisis, both domestically and professionally. Jessie's leg continued to pain her, and the health of neither Borys nor John was good. On the promise of his next novel, another tale of anarchists in the successful vein of *The Secret Agent*, his long-suffering agent J.B. Pinker had advanced him a good deal of money, but Conrad kept being sidetracked by other projects, including a series of reminiscences for a journal edited by Ford and the magnificent story 'The secret sharer'. Tensions between Pinker and Conrad were building. When Pinker demanded to see his work on the anarchist novel, Conrad threatened to throw it in the fire. He finally delivered the manuscript in January 1910, but the meeting resulted in an enormous row, almost terminal for their friendship (Pinker accused him of being unable to speak English). Ford meanwhile had begun a complicated affair, was estranged from his wife and behaving erratically, and Conrad quarrelled with him too, breaking off contact for two years.

The stress was too much for Conrad's weak constitution, and he suffered a total breakdown. He lay in bed, feverish, rambling mainly in Polish, except to curse Pinker, for three months. His friends, including Pinker, rallied round, and as he regained strength he revised the manuscript of his novel, now called *Under Western Eyes*, which finally appeared in late 1911. He lived quietly for the next few years, publishing memoirs based on the articles for Ford,[9] and making more literary acquaintances, including André Gide, Richard Curle (who would write the first book-length study of Conrad)[10] and Bertrand Russell.

The publication of *Chance* in 1914 was a turning-point in Conrad's career. It was the beginning of his literary decline, but it did make him, for the first time in his life at 56, financially secure and independent. He felt able to take his family to Poland for the first time, his own first visit since 1893, but the First World War broke out while he was there, and getting back to Britain was complicated; upon his return he sank once more into depression. Nevertheless, more works appeared. *Victory* (1915) is a strange and romantic Malay tale in which an island idyll is shattered by the appearance of three fugitives; *The Shadow-Line* (1917) another sea-story, emphasises the mutual interdependence of captain and crew; *The Arrow of Gold* (1919) romanticises his Marseilles days in a tale of running guns for the doomed Carlist rebels in Spain. Now a celebrity, he did minor war work, fund-raising, visiting naval bases and writing articles; he also relinquished his civil list pension, of £100 per annum, which he had been awarded in 1910. Most tragically, his son Borys was gassed and left shell-shocked as part of the final offensive of the war, a month before the armistice. The poor man was profoundly affected, and his reintegration into civilian life consequently troubled.

Conrad and Jessie, neither of them well, gained a reputation of being reclusive, but there were still plenty of visits from literary types, and his public standing continued to increase. A trip to America in 1923 was a triumph; he sat for many portraits, including a bust by Epstein; he turned down a knighthood and several honorary degrees, including one from Cambridge University; more critical studies of his work appeared; he found unexpected sources of income from the sale of his early manuscripts, releases of limited edition pamphlets repackaging earlier essays and plays, and film rights (Conrad lived to see the first film of his work, Maurice Tourneur's *Victory*). He was able to indulge his liking for engineering. He and John built complex Meccano structures and collected miniature steam engines. He was now able to splash out on cars, and bought himself a Cadillac, which he adored but drove too fast. Long in planning, *The Rescue* finally appeared in 1920, followed in 1923 by *The*

[9]   Published as *A Personal Record*.
[10]   Richard Curle, *Joseph Conrad: A Study*, New York: Doubleday, Page and Company, 1914, still a valuable work.

Rover, set in post-revolutionary France. This was his last completed novel, and explored themes of identity, community, isolation and political action. The book is a slow, dark one, with a — for Conrad — straightforward narrative style which meant that it suffered at the hands of critics (ironically given Conrad's pioneering modernist work) in comparison to the new masters of modernism such as James Joyce and Virginia Woolf.

His health continued to decline; Epstein found him ill and crotchety, and he suffered from rheumatism and asthma. In August 1924, he died at his desk suddenly, from a heart attack, leaving an unfinished novel *Suspense*. He had been a writer for thirty years.

Politics and literature

This is not fundamentally a book about literature, but politics. Some think it is a mistake to read works of literature for the odd political nugget that can be mined from them.[11] I disagree. Some writers write deliberately political books, others write about politics as a backdrop to their drama, while others, either ignorant or uncaring of political issues, provide fascinating insights into the assumptions of their day. Conrad was very much of the first group, and often in the second as well. Always alert, intelligent, ironic and sceptical, his is fine political commentary.

I certainly do not wish to suggest that he had a worked-out political system in his head (or, if he had had, that that would be where the chief interest in his work would lie). Neither do I want to claim that *Almayer's Folly* is politically indistinguishable from *The Rover*. And, of course, just because a character in a novel — even Marlow, a narrator Conrad used on four separate occasions — says something, that does not mean that Conrad says (is asserting) it.

The relationship between political writing and literature is problematic. George Orwell's work, for instance, falls short of being first-rate literature, but the excellence of his work showcases the straightforward pithiness of his messages — or is it the other way around? Aldous Huxley's novels are less good as literature, and certainly much less sensible in the round, but *Brave New World* carries an intellectual punch that Orwell's work, even in *Nineteen Eighty-Four* or *Animal Farm*, doesn't quite match.

With regard to Conrad, there is much of interest, politically, in his later work, in *The Rover*, say, or *The Shadow-Line*, but these are gener-

[11] E.g. Richard A. Posner, 'Orwell versus Huxley: economics, technology, privacy and satire', *Philosophy and Literature*, 24, 2000, 1-33.

ally weaker. For the record, I subscribe to the so-called achievement-and-decline thesis[12] which sees Conrad's career as reaching a peak with *Under Western Eyes*, and then tailing off gradually following his breakdown of 1910. This view isn't particularly fashionable today, it should be added.[13] What is true, however, is that the major political statements, sentiments and descriptions do seem to appear in his greatest works by and large: *Nostromo*, 'Heart of darkness', *The Secret Agent*, *The Nigger of the "Narcissus"* and *Under Western Eyes*. These magnificent novels are at the focal point of the Conradian picture, though, as with Orwell, whether it is their magnificence that fosters their political profundity, or vice versa, is a question best left to the critics to disentangle.

He was not a very exceptional or unusual man, in the way that Byron or Malcolm Lowry were. Neither was he much of a performer, in the way of a Norman Mailer or a Martin Amis. Had he been born a hundred years later, would he have coped terribly well on television, with his odd English and his reactionary opinions? One suspects not. But, for a literary figure, he had unusually wide experience. He had been involved, indirectly, in revolutionary struggles in Poland and Spain. He had worked, with his hands, and in a team, for several years. He knew poverty and illness. When he speaks of the world—of his world—he knows what he is talking about. He knew about the Belgian exploitation of the Congo, because he had seen it, and he knew what it is like to fight a typhoon in East Asia.

None of that makes his political judgement perfect, by any means —and of course he often wrote about things with which he was not familiar or comfortable. He was not a sage. What I hope to do in this book is to look at a few of the big themes of 21st century thought and politics, and try to see them through Conrad's eyes. We will find that, more often than not, Conrad can be a striking, sometimes depressing, commentator. But if his descriptions of darkness are paradoxically enlightening, then maybe a little depression—shall we say *realism*?—is a price worth paying.

[12] Thomas C. Moser, *Joseph Conrad: Achievement and Decline*, Cambridge, MA: Harvard University Press, 1957.
[13] Gary Geddes, *Conrad's Later Novels*, Montreal: McGill-Queen's University Press, 1980.

Chapter Two

The Big Themes: Imperialism, Racism, Globalisation

Conrad on empire

Conrad's career began with a series of works about empire. His first two novels, *Almayer's Folly* and *An Outcast of the Islands*, dealt directly with the plight of the colonial masters in what is now Indonesia. This is surprising at first sight: surely the 'plight' was of the colonised peoples. However, Conrad had experienced the gap between rhetoric and reality of the 'white man's burden' at first hand, and was keen to explain the terrible effects it had on the 'masters'—a similar message to Orwell's brilliant essay 'Shooting an elephant.' He chronicled the complex interplay between ideology and circumstance, and, even in his first writings, the often painful results of differing perceptions of power and legitimacy.

Of his direct experiences of being an imperial subject in Poland we have to look primarily at his autobiographical and non-fiction works; his episodic memoir *A Personal Record* contains a good deal of material about his morbid early years. Conrad's view of power politics was coloured by his own past: Russia, and to a lesser extent Prussia, were the villains. His novels of European revolution, *The Secret Agent* and *Under Western Eyes*, assume the villainy of the Russian state as a given.

His time in the Congo was painful and distressing, and he wrote much less on Africa than on the East, but what he did write—a novella, a short story and a co-written novel—were devastating. Enough has been written about 'Heart of darkness' to fill a small library, but we shouldn't forget his early (1897) story 'An outpost of progress', a deeply ironic title. 'Outpost' is a black comedy, and with wonderfully measured sarcasm, Conrad later wrote of the story as being "the lightest part of the loot I carried off from Central Africa" (a throwaway line echoing the pungent words of one of his final essays in which he calls the 'opening' of Africa "the vilest scramble for loot that ever disfigured the history of human conscience"[1]), but it does not spare the colonialist ideology or rhetoric. *The Inheritors* (1901), a more overtly satirical and political work largely written by Ford Madox Ford, sent up King Leopold as the egregious Duc de Mersch, whose mission to civilise the Arctic regions was "nothing more nor less than a corporate exploitation of unhappy Esquimaux". And his more personal opinion is on the record in letters written to anti-imperialism campaigner Sir Roger Casement towards the end of 1903.

The imperial ideal

But for all that, critical opinion is divided. Conrad lived in the greatest imperial nation of them all, and seemed to share at least some of the popular enthusiasm for empire. His work abounds with the trappings of imperial fiction, where the hero tests himself against danger, alone, in unknown and unfamiliar surroundings. The genre was exciting and dramatic, congruent with a particular view of the 'imperial adventure'. The hero has to be established as such, and the (white, European, usually male) readers would expect to read about white males. The unfamiliar surroundings were the mysterious jungles of Africa, exotic India, pitiless deserts, tropical islands. It was an unEnglish world of earthquakes, hurricanes, sandstorms, floods and fever, and the empire provided a colourful panoply of murderous subjects, thugees, Hashashin, Pathan cutthroats, assegai-wielding Zulus, whirling dervishes and Polynesian maneaters. In an adventure story, heroism is reinforced by the evil intent of the 'other'; if the hero, however brave and resourceful, is merely slaughtering legitimate representatives of a valuable, if alien, culture, in order to support an unmotivated transfer of resources from that culture to a richer, more powerful one (a more usual view of the imperial enterprise today), then it is harder to take his heroism at face value.

Conrad wrote stories of adventure giving men the opportunities to test themselves and become heroes—a classic imperialist trope. This, together with his Anglophilia and his relative lack of interest in

---

[1]   From 'Geography and some explorers'.

'native' cultures, has led a number of critics to argue that his view is basically a conservative, pro-English view. It was easy enough to dissociate himself from the *excesses* of imperialism; Leopold was Belgian after all, while in Britain, even the most imperialist Prime Minister of all, Lord Salisbury, detested the jingoism that grew up about the empire.[2] But many have argued that Conrad was still an imperialist at heart, if an intelligent and realistic one. Certainly his treatment of the Chinese coolies in 'Typhoon', to take one example, hardly credits them with a great deal of autonomy and sophistication — they are just another part of the hostile environment — and this is not an isolated case. Furthermore, Conrad is on record, in a number of letters, of saying approving things about the British Empire, and seems to have regarded it as uniquely well-motivated; most of the immoral imperialists in his work are from continental Europe. If one reads the critics, one can discern three Conrads: the conservative imperialist, the sceptical imperialist and the anti-imperialist — and this difference of opinion goes back to the original critical reception of 'Heart of darkness'.[3]

It is important to realise that Conrad, although he is certainly guilty on occasion of simplifying and reifying the perspectives of entire cultures, never subscribed to a crude Manichaean vision. His first two novels were his least subtle in terms of characterisation, but cannot be accused of privileging the perceptions of the eponymous white characters. Both novels were set in Sambir, a fictional settlement in Borneo (now in Indonesia), where adventurer Tom Lingard has set up an outpost of his trading company. Lingard is English, but the territory is administered by Holland. Almayer and Willems, the major protagonists of *Almayer's Folly* and *An Outcast of the Islands* respectively, are both Dutch, but Almayer's wife is a Sulu pirate's daughter orphaned and adopted by Lingard and 'given' to Almayer by him, while the tiny village of Sambir contains many social groups, from native Dyaks and Malay royalty to the ubiquitous Chinese immigrants and Arab traders.

This is not a homogeneous world — there are several viewpoints depicted. No one picture can claim primacy; the plots are of unceasing struggles for power driven by thoughts of gain. Despite the many conflicts across racial and cultural divides, Conrad is not

[2]   Andrew Roberts, *Salisbury: Victorian Titan*, London: Weidenfeld & Nicolson, 1999, 178, 518.

[3]   See the contemporary reviews collected in Norman Sherry (ed.), *Conrad: The Critical Heritage*, Routledge & Kegan Paul: London, 1973.

describing anything like what Samuel Huntington has called the clash of civilisations.[4] This is an area where the goals and desires of many of the actors, though culturally embedded, are not culturally determined, and where the blithe assumptions of moral superiority of the white men are portrayed with Conrad's trademark irony. Although the white men are the main focus of psychological interest, we see Sambir from several perspectives, perhaps most powerfully that of Babalatchi, politician and former pirate. Almayer and Willems are allowed to speak for themselves, and manage only to condemn themselves through their own mouths. A drunken argument between the two of them ends with "the two specimens of the superior race glar[ing] at each other savagely".

The assumption that particular types of misbehaviour are peculiar to the developing world is not a type of crassness unique to the 19th century. In April 2007 it was discovered the President of the World Bank, Paul Wolfowitz, who was heading a drive against corruption in its debtor states, had engineered a transfer for his girlfriend to the US State Department, where she was on a salary larger than that of the Secretary of State Condoleezza Rice. Wolfowitz defended his actions, but it is not clear if he would have done the same had the imbroglio concerned, say, a government minister in Nigeria. At the same time, scandal engulfed Randall Tobias, United States Director of Foreign Assistance. US government aid comes with many strings attached, and in the fight against AIDS these can be extremely unhelpful when they are pulled by the religious and evangelical right. In particular, groups funded by the US must oppose prostitution explicitly, and a third of the money disbursed by the President's Emergency Plan for AIDS Relief must be spent on encouraging chastity as a method of prevention. Whether or not this is a sensible method of getting AIDS relief to the people who really need it, it became less credible when Tobias was forced to resign after admitting patronising an escort service run by a woman under investigation for running a prostitution business. Meanwhile, all, especially the British government, are agreed that bribery is a terrible drag on the economies of the developing world, which makes one wonder why it halted an investigation into allegations that BAE Systems, a British defence contractor, had bribed Saudi Arabian officials.

Despite their assumption of superiority, neither Willems nor Almayer is much to write home about, and neither is the sort of rep-

---

[4]   Samuel P. Huntington, *The Clash of Civilizations and the Remaking of World Order*, London: Simon & Schuster, 1997.

resentative of the imperial adventure to excite the boys reading their adventure stories. In *An Outcast of the Islands*, Willems jumps ship in the East. Lingard finds him a job with a merchant, which he loses when he is caught stealing to pay gambling debts; Lingard helps him again by putting him under Almayer in Sambir, but here Willems comes under the spell of Aïssa, who leads him to betray Lingard's secret knowledge about the river passage to the interior. Willems is robustly villainous, but amoral. Rather than purely evil, he is an inveterate myth-maker, who forsakes the comforting social support of 'white' society, preferring in Sambir the company of a ragtag band of superannuated Malay pirates. Willems is one of the most racist characters in Conrad's *oeuvre*, feeling for the "miserable savages … all the hate of his race, his morality, his intelligence." "He was so civilised!" But his need for a white identity, and the feeling of superiority over the various non-white people of Sambir, "quickens as his personal identity falls from his grasp and he finds his actual and psychic space increasingly restricted."[5] The degradation of Willems shows how hard it is to construct oneself unsupported by the scaffolding of community, workmates or morals.

Almayer, the focus of *Almayer's Folly*, set some fifteen years or so after the events of *Outcast*, is a very different kettle of fish. Several years on, his marriage to the Sulu woman 'given' to him by Lingard has soured, and feeling desperately in need of the support and status that his Dutch ancestry should give him, he acts out the rituals that he perceives essential for the 'white' life (he is the only white man in Sambir). Conrad's evocation brilliantly moves between Almayer's desperate need for solidarity, and the egotism associated with it. There is nothing wrong with pride in Dutch ancestry of course, but there is something corrupting about the belief that it makes one automatically superior to the non-white native dwellers. Almayer's pride is made more painful by the guilt of having married outside his caste; this guilt he hopes to expiate by giving his half-caste daughter Nina a 'European' education in Singapore while he makes his fortune (a forlorn obsession), afterwards taking her back to live a 'proper' life in Europe.

Nina has other ideas. Back in Sambir, now a young woman, it is her Malay heritage that begins to predominate over her European inheritance. Eventually, her identity as an Asian woman cannot be suppressed any longer, and she escapes with a Balinese prince on the

[5] As pointed out by J.H. Stape, 'Introduction' in Joseph Conrad, *An Outcast of the Islands*, Oxford: Oxford University Press, 1992, xi–xxiii, at xv.

run from the Dutch authorities. Almayer is appalled and gives chase, but when he catches them he merely discovers the depth of Nina's love. Although he believes that Nina will be ill-treated — "For he is a savage. Between him and you there is a barrier that nothing can remove" — Nina retorts that the same barrier exists between herself and her father. In the end, Almayer, broken, cannot bear the thought of "white men finding my daughter with this Malay," and prefers instead to aid their escape. As Nina and her lover sail away, "he fell on his hands and knees, and, creeping along the sand, erased carefully with his hand all traces of Nina's footsteps. He piled up small heaps of sand, leaving behind him a line of miniature graves right down to the water." The imperial ideal has given Almayer very little and he retires into drug-induced oblivion. It has raised his hopes, sustained him through a life of crushing futility and loneliness, and left him bereft. The supposed superiority of the only white man on Sambir is phoney, rooted in rituals of behaviour and empty assertion.

Conrad teases out a number of different imperial conceptions in his work. He excoriates the Congolese venture as little more than plunder decorated with pious words (a minority view but not a unique one — Bismarck once annotated a document setting out Leopold's supposed anti-slavery programme with the single word "Schwindel"), but he is aware that there is a space for an imperial project that genuinely attempts to provide better conditions for the 'natives', represented as being unable to pursue (either through impotence or ignorance) their own interests. Again such a position is not the prerogative of the European colonists of the 19th and early 20th centuries. Even now there are many projects, supported by left and right, which share this 'imperial' form, from George Bush's now-abandoned attempts to bring democracy to the Middle East, to left wing protests against globalisation, to campaigns to empower women, to peacekeeping, to attempts to foster free market institutions in the developing world, to the interventions of NGOs, to attempts by European and American members of the Anglican communion to persuade African churches to tone down their homophobia. All assume hegemony of moral codes rooted in the Western world. Robin Cook's misguided attempt to intervene in the India/Pakistan dispute over Kashmir in 1997 was angrily rejected by India, and was motivated by a clearly imperial set of assumptions, that the UK (unlike India and Pakistan) would be a fair dealer, even-handed, rational and unhampered by years of ideological and historical baggage. Such assumptions may be true — similar interventions by Norway in the Israel/Palestine dispute, and the civil war in Sri Lanka, had some positive impact, if ultimately unsuccessfully — but are imperial nonetheless. And none of the examples mentioned in this paragraph is obviously self-serving.

Conrad himself was aware of the difficulties, indeterminacies and complexities in trying to pin down a single motive for an action, even though he was inclined to be cynical. As he wrote in *The Secret Agent*, "The way of even the most justifiable revolutions is prepared by personal impulses disguised into creeds." He was also aware that it was the fine words in particular that made the imperial project possible, made it into an admirable thing to do, rather than "a squeeze, and nothing more." Marlow, the narrator of 'Heart of darkness', explains in a famous passage: "The conquest of the earth, which mostly means the taking it away from those who have a different complexion or slightly flatter noses than ourselves, is not a pretty thing when you look at it too much. What redeems it is the idea only. An idea at the back of it, not a sentimental pretence but an idea; and an unselfish belief in the idea."

'Heart of darkness' is a key exploration of this view, but it is given its most concrete form in the savagely comic story 'An outpost of progress', in which Kayerts and Carlier, useless representatives of a trading company, run a jungle station together with a Sierra Leonean clerk called Makola who actually does all the work. In this alien environment they are "like blind men in a dark room, aware only of what came into contact with them ... but unable to see the general aspect of things." While Makola bargains with native tribesmen, the two look "down on proceedings, understanding nothing", laughing at what they see as the funny-looking natives. When they do befriend a local tribesman, it is only to indulge him irresponsibly. "They returned [his affection] in a way. Carlier slapped him on the back, and recklessly struck off matches for his amusement. Kayerts was always ready to let him have a sniff of the ammonia bottle."

Kayerts and Carlier are also in nominal charge of ten local workmen for the station, though they cannot get decent work out of them. When the workmen all disappear, the two are initially upset — "We took care of them as if they had been our children" — and then annoyed — "the ungrateful brutes." But when Makola shows up with six magnificent elephant tusks, they realise that he has sold the workmen to slave traders. "We can't touch [the ivory], of course" says Kayerts, "slavery is an awful thing." The impersonal narrator of the story allows that "they believed their words." But when they see Makola going through the bureaucratic processes of weighing and storing the enormous tusks they help him — "it's deplorable, but, the men being Company's men the ivory is Company's ivory." They blame Makola, and gradually decide that there is little they can do — which is certainly true, there is no possibility of getting the men back — and in the end decide to be silent. They use the Company as an excuse; no-one would thank them for raising the difficult issue. Their end, of course, is sticky, an ignoble one for "two pioneers of trade and progress." The rhetoric of the colonial project is rehearsed in various places through the story, but Kayerts and Carlier are the reality; one a soldier, one a bureaucrat, leaving behind misery and conflict, contributing little beyond idleness, incompetence and litter.

The end of 'Outpost' is ambiguous. Kayerts and Carlier are incapable of bringing the benefits of European civilisation to Africa, and Conrad is sceptical of the imperial enterprise being able to motivate officials and administrators capable of carrying out an enlightened programme. But if such administrators could be found, would the enterprise be legitimate? This is a pressing question even now. Non-governmental organisations and aid agencies have developed structures that reduce the incentives for those from the 'enlightened' North to despoil those they have taken under their wing, but, as William Easterly has recently argued,[6] the result is often to entrench the power of local strongmen with no obvious benefit to the locals.

Kurtz

'Heart of darkness' tells a more pungent tale than 'Outpost', as Marlow narrates his own experiences with an African trading company sailing down a mighty river. Marlow is a fascinating narrator, changed by the events in the tale, perhaps even changed by the experience of telling (in one of Conrad's complex narratorial relationships, Marlow's narration of the tale is itself narrated for us, the readers, by one of a group of listeners). The key event from Marlow's point of view is his quest for Kurtz; but the point of the story, filtered through Marlow's direct and reported experiences, is Kurtz himself.

Kurtz works for the company, based at the Inner Station up river, as an ivory trader. He has a reputation as an exceptional man, des-

[6]   William Easterly, *The White Man's Burden: Why the West's Efforts to Aid the Rest Have Done So Much Ill and So Little Good*, New York: The Penguin Press, 2006.

tined for great things in the administration. He is the man to supply the idea to support the imperial project.

> 'He is a prodigy,' [the brickmaker] said at last. 'He is an emissary of pity, and science, and progress, and devil knows what else. We want,' he began to declaim suddenly, 'for the guidance of the cause entrusted to us by Europe, so to speak, higher intelligence, wide sympathies, a singleness of purpose.'

He writes poetry, plays music, paints, is multi-lingual and his eloquence and intensity mean that he "would have been a splendid leader of an extreme party." He represents the peak of European sensibility and culture. "All Europe contributed to the making of Kurtz." But he has gone missing, and Marlow is sent to bring him back. As Marlow travels up the river, he sees increasingly many signs of the degradation of the colonial ideal, and develops a longing to hear Kurtz's voice justifying and explaining the brutal and often mystifying endeavour.

Away from his European roots, there is little to restrain Kurtz. He has technological power over the natives. He has the resources of a thousand years of European culture and history behind him. The dark, uncivilised continent is a *tabula rasa* on which Kurtz can write the ultimate human poem; he can bring enlightenment, single-handed, on his own terms, to whole societies.

But he brings a hell on Earth. It is known that many Europeans in Africa reverted to savagery—James Sligo Jameson paid six handkerchiefs to be allowed to watch (and sketch) a young slave girl being sacrificed and eaten, while Léon Rom decorated his flower bed with 21 human heads he had had severed.[7] Conrad may or may not have been aware of such real-life figures, but he knew that they were a pathology of the imperial psychology. The Faustian Kurtz is in total control, without restraint, and unable to resist taking part in "unspeakable rites" with sacrifices offered up to him.

His decline is charted in a pamphlet he has written for the International Society for the Suppression of Savage Customs, which expresses his ideals for improvement of the natives, and shrewdly shows what leverage white men may exploit. Marlow recalls his discovery of the pamphlet ironically.

> The opening paragraph, however, in the light of later information, strikes me now as ominous. He began with the argument that we whites, from the point of development we had arrived at, 'must necessarily appear to them [savages] in the nature of

[7]   Adam Hochschild, *King Leopold's Ghost*, Boston: Houghton Mifflin, 1998.

supernatural beings—we approach them with the might as of a deity,' and so on, and so on. 'By the simple exercise of our will we can exert a power for good practically unbounded,' etc. etc. ... There were no practical hints to interrupt the magic current of phrases, unless a kind of note at the foot of the last page, scrawled evidently much later in an unsteady hand, may be regarded as the exposition of a method. It was very simple and at the end of that moving appeal to every altruistic sentiment it blazed at you luminous and terrifying like a flash of lightning in a serene sky: 'Exterminate all the brutes!'

Once one has appeared as a God, "with thunder and lightning, you know" (i.e. superior weaponry), one needs to behave as a God in order to preserve one's position (this is what Almayer, out of weakness, and Willems, thanks to love, cannot do). One might hope to do good, to improve one's worshippers, but one is likely to end up being a God first and an improver second (since the latter is dependent on the former). When Marlow finally finds Kurtz's station, he discovers that it is surrounded by six posts ornamented by human heads.

Idealism is important, and it may be that a display of power is required to allow beneficial ideals to be applied practically, but events are often such that the 'shock and awe' needs constant attention and the ideals are never implemented. In the end, the power becomes an end in itself. A bank robber will use as much violence as will achieve his purpose, but an improver's work is never completed. The imperial adventure was not the first time in history that this had happened, and as recent events in the Middle East have shown, it was not the last. It was a lack of available restraint, the need to display power and the inability to find reverse gear that led to the abuses of Abu Ghraib and Guantánamo, and even in 2007 one in three American soldiers serving in Iraq thought that torture was justified in some circumstances, and fewer than half felt that noncombatants should be treated with dignity and respect, as required by the Geneva Conventions.[8] Nevertheless, it goes without saying that the Americans are certainly not the worst offenders here. For exhibitions of savagery in service of idealism, al Qaeda and various elements of the Iraqi insurgency take some beating.

Kurtz's idealism is as important as his genius, and Conrad does not depict his genius terribly convincingly—it is asserted rather more than demonstrated. In Coppola's film *Apocalypse Now*, an entertaining cross between 'Heart of darkness' and *M*A*S*H*, Kurtz is transmuted into an American general in Vietnam, so his genius is

[8]   'Contaminated', *The Economist*, 12th May, 2007.

represented by his stellar army record (and his portrayal by super-star Marlon Brando). But the corresponding weakness of the film is that it is hard to imagine what Kurtz's idealism could possibly consist in other than madness. An American general driven by dreams of bringing enlightenment to the natives must be mad already, because that is not what generals do. Viewers of the movie are not surprised that Kurtz has produced a killing field, because what else (realistically) would an idealistic general produce? Conrad's story is at its weakest while building Kurtz up, but more effectively dramatises the gap between ideal and reality.

In such a position, momentum is all. Kurtz needs to feel the possibility of progress in order to justify the savagery in the context of his idealism. But he is ill, and desperate to secure his idealistic legacy. He dies in a moment of "intense and hopeless despair" and then comes his famous last cry: "The horror! The horror!" There has been much debate over its significance, or even whether it has a significance, but surely the weight of the violence and inhumanity, at the point at which all possibility of achievement of the ideals underlying them has disappeared, and with it any further illusion that he was doing any kind of good, must have been overwhelming. Savage customs were not suppressed; all that was left was the horror. Kurtz's last moment was a terrible one, and although it is possible to detect some sort of redemptive power in his cry, it cannot have been much more than a simple realisation of the dreadful facts.

Racism

Conrad was a European writer at the turn of the 20th century. In a sense, racism was the linguistic, social and psychological small change of the day, and we cannot expect Conrad to transcend his times any more than we can expect Mallory or Austen or Amis to. Perhaps the most obvious linguistic nod to racism is Conrad's frequent use of the word 'nigger', which would clearly be unacceptable today without a good deal of contextualisation. He does not use the word casually; even at the time it was thought offensive, and he used it when he wanted a harsh word. The title of *The Nigger of the "Narcissus"* was deliberately bleak and shocking, and when his American publishers changed the title to *The Children of the Sea*, he agreed only under protest (he later called the alternative title "absurdly sweet"). The use of the term to refer to James Wait is not neutral — during the course of the novel Wait himself protests against the term: "You wouldn't call me nigger if I wasn't half dead, you Irish beggar!"

There are several other examples where Conrad exploits the shocking quality of racist language; for instance, in *Under Western Eyes* the elderly English narrator feels he has to explain and decode Razumov's angry anti-Semitic abuse of Laspara.

Conrad's perceptions are certainly not those of today — Wait's response is no less racist — but it is not clear that he should be condemned for that. To insist that someone celebrating his 150th birthday should have anticipated our enlightened views, and to insist that any moral consensus we happen to have reached is a clear example of progress, is to succumb to yet another brand of imperialism, a temporal variety.

If Conrad's language is sometimes obviously racist, then it also has to be admitted that many of the things he says are straightforwardly opposed to racism. Again, 'Heart of darkness' is the main text here, but many of Conrad's tales include explicit statements that white men are not superior to others, and that their exploitation of others' resources and territory are not justified by their technological and economic superiority, their supposed good intentions, or the supposed savagery of the native inhabitants. Willems, Almayer, Kayerts and Carlier, imperialists all, are hardly the superior beings they consider themselves to be, while the narrator Marlow peppers 'Heart of darkness' with vivid vignettes of injustice, exploited workers and abandoned bodies. He can see no rationale for conquest beyond the surface physiognomical differences between the races.

The view of Conrad as good-hearted if roughly expressive, prevailed until a powerful intervention in 1975 from Nigerian novelist and future Nobel Prizewinner Chinua Achebe, who undid the consensus and called Conrad a "bloody racist." Achebe accepted that Conrad was not charitable to the Europeans in 'Heart of darkness', but that was not the point. Conrad, said Achebe, saw Africa as "a metaphysical battlefield devoid of all recognizable humanity, into which the wandering European enters at his peril." He was appalled at the dehumanisation of Africa and Africans implied by that attitude.[9]

---

[9]   Chinua Achebe, 'An image of Africa: racism in Conrad's *Heart of Darkness*', in Joseph Conrad, *Heart of Darkness*, 3rd Norton Critical Edition, ed. Robert Kimbrough, New York: W.W. Norton & Company Ltd, 1988, 251-262. This edition includes three responses as well as Achebe's famous paper itself, on top of several valuable resources about Conrad's time in Africa, notably 'The Congo diary' and 'The Up-river book', and the writing of 'Heart of darkness'.

Others chipped in. Frances B. Singh argued that "Marlow's sympathy for the blacks is only superficial. He feels sorry for them when he sees them dying, but when he sees them healthy, practising their customs, he feels nothing but abhorrence and loathing, like a good colonizer to whom such a feeling offers a perfect rationalization for his policies."[10] Singh accepts that Marlow and Conrad may well have different views, that Conrad's views cannot simply be 'read off' from Marlow's, but many of Marlow's judgements are echoed in Conrad's letters and non-fiction. Singh also acquits Conrad of the charge of bad faith; she sees him as a man of his times, unable to transcend their limitations but equally sincere in his rejection of imperialism. But ultimately, "for the modern reader his limitations reduce the significance of his achievement as a psychologist and a moralist, ironically turning the story that was meant to be a clear-cut attack on a vicious system into a partial apology for it."

These are not charges that can be dismissed out of hand, but ultimately, as argued above, we must be wary of imposing unreasonable demands on people who are remote from us in time or culture. Furthermore, much of the discussion is premised on the grand narrative developed as a result of the branch of critical theory called 'post-colonial studies', which tries to show that the colonial 'other' is constructed by Western writers from a Eurocentric bias, that European culture assumes itself to be 'normal' and 'rational', and that other cultures (however valid) are departures from those standards of normality. We need not follow the often impenetrable fads and jargon of critical theory for our purposes here; suffice it to say that the central charge against Conrad is that Africans are essentially "props" (Achebe's word) in the background of the central drama in his work, which concerns the failure of certain aspects of European thought and civilisation. To an extent that charge is justified.

Marlow's narrative certainly portrays the African jungle as a place of danger, and that is not simply because of the natural environment; for him, it was "the gleam of fires, the throb of drums, the drone of weird incantations ... [which] had beguiled [Kurtz's] unlawful soul beyond the bounds of permitted aspirations." He is not interested in the content of the incantations, or of any of the myriad social relations that obtained in African societies at the time; instead he dwells on the effects of the sounds of one type of interaction on "one petty European" (Achebe's phrase). This indifference to the host culture is

---

[10]   Frances B. Singh, 'The colonialistic bias of *Heart of Darkness*' in Kimbrough, *Heart of Darkness*, 268-280.

not a single blind spot for Conrad; although his Malay novels include much detail about Sambir, and many Malay characters are key actors in their plots, it was spotted early on by those in the know that Conrad's portrayal of Malay society was not terribly accurate.

But ultimately, Conrad is a European writer. He was certainly interested in many aspects of the experience of being colonised — he was, after all, from a colonised nation, and his parents had died as a direct result of his father's rebellion against the Russian overlords. But he was also interested in European thought and civilisation; his readers would be overwhelmingly European. If imperialism was to be ended, or at least transformed and made more humane, changing European attitudes was an important step. On a practical level, Conrad de-glamorised the empire; with the possible exception of *Lord Jim*, his work is unremittingly negative about the effects of empire on colonised and colonisers alike.

There is, however, an ambiguity. The modern insight — and it *is* a genuine insight, not just fashionable ideology — is that imperialism, however well-intentioned, entrenches racial inequalities. Conrad certainly argues that imperialism as he had witnessed it, remote from the humbug of good intentions, was a bad thing. Did he also imply that imperialism was *necessarily* a bad thing, even if the intentions were good and genuine? That is a harder question. Nevertheless, there is some evidence that Conrad was at least moving toward such a conclusion.

On a deeper level, Conrad laid bare the contradictions underlying justificatory European ideologies. 'An outpost of progress' and *Almayer's Folly* show how poorly those ideologies were applied. 'Heart of darkness' and *An Outcast of the Islands* shows how inadequate they were, and how, were they applied effectively, they would be even more corrupting than the "scramble for loot" that actually ensued. To address this deeper level, Conrad's gaze was primarily on the Europeans. Achebe tacitly assumes that to write about the missing heart of the European soul, the emptiness at the centre of Enlightenment in the context of the imperial venture (the context where, as Conrad and others such as John Gray have argued,[11] the Enlightenment story breaks down most radically) demands an anthropological understanding of African society that would certainly have been beyond most authors in the 19th century, and indeed most Western authors in the 21st. Even today, the most-read

[11]   See John Gray, *Heresies: Against Progress and Other Illusions*, London: Granta, 2004, especially 104-106.

works about a Sub-Saharan culture are the series of novels about the *No. 1 Ladies' Detective Agency*, written by a Scottish (white, male) Professor of Medical Law.

Parenthetically, we might also point out that a recent slew of Hollywood films has portrayed Africa in more sophisticated terms than is usual in that part of California, with a series of thoughtful stories, big budgets, big stars and gritty depictions of the refugee camps, famine and Western meddling taken from our news bulletins. The realism is certainly greater than earlier American efforts like *Call Me Bwana* or *Out of Africa*. But the films—think of *Hotel Rwanda*, *Lord of War*, *The Constant Gardener*, *The Last King of Scotland* and *Blood Diamond*—do not seem to be much of an advance on 'Heart of darkness' in terms of cultural understanding. Only *Hotel Rwanda* dares boast a black lead. The other four stories are told through the eyes of white visitors to the continent, and the reason for that is that studios would be much less likely to invest in, and Western audiences much less likely to watch, a film about Africans (of the five, only *The Last King of Scotland* took less at the box office than *Hotel Rwanda*). What Conrad called "material interests" strike again. But it is worth pointing out that it is asking a lot for Conrad to have achieved in 1899 what sophisticated film-makers could not in 2006, especially when the film-makers were in receipt of the wisdom of post-colonial critics while Conrad was not.

Actually, as Marlow makes clear (and 'An outpost of progress' even clearer), the European experience in Africa *was* one of dealing with a shadowy place with which interaction was extremely difficult. To borrow an image from modern science, Africa is less the heart of darkness than dark matter, a cosmological concept of matter that is of unknown composition and cannot be observed directly; its presence can only be inferred from its gravitational effects on visible matter. The European experience of Africa was somewhat like that; the social structures that Europeans wished to find were not there, and were created—but African society, as Conrad is well aware, carried on in the interstices, while European-style institutions remained hollow.

"We were cut off from the comprehension of our surroundings; we glided past like phantoms, wondering and secretly appalled, as sane men would be before an enthusiastic outbreak in a madhouse." The Europeans did not understand African customs, and thereby assumed they were driven by irrationality, but in this quote, is Conrad (or Marlow) *really* assuming that Africans are mad, as

opposed to anticipating Foucault's point that madness is a construction of 'sane' society?[12] The key phrase here, I suggest, is not the
image of the madhouse (or many of the images of ugliness and mon-
strosity that follow in the next few pages), but rather that "we glided
past like phantoms". Phantoms are monstrosities in themselves, and
also have the properties of dark matter; the imagery is even-handed,
but Marlow, as a European, describes only the Europeans' view.
Conrad the author unconsciously backs up Marlow's stance by
removing African voices from the narrative altogether. He does not
(and, according to many cultural relativists, cannot) know what the
Africans felt about the Europeans, although he knows more than
enough about human nature to make a guess. There is similar imagery in *Victory*, where the villains of the story see "native life as a mere
play of shadows," and Heyst's Chinese manservant appears and disappears in a ghostly fashion; meanwhile, in *The Shadow-Line*, "The
very gang of yellow coolies busy about the main hatch was less substantial than the stuff dreams were made of. For who on earth would
dream of Chinamen? ..."[13] This view also appears in Conrad's
non-fiction, where his essay '"Well done"' describes the lack of interaction between the Europeans and the "ghostlike" Chinese sailors.

In this context, how powerful becomes the image of the French
man-of-war that Marlow sees on his way to the Congo.

> For a time I would feel I belonged still to a world of straightfor-
> ward facts; but the feeling would not last long. Something would
> turn up to scare it away. Once, I remember, we came upon a
> man-of-war anchored off the coast. There wasn't even a shed
> there and she was shelling the bush. It appears the French had
> one of their wars going on thereabouts. Her ensign drooped limp
> like a rag, the muzzles of the long six-inch guns stuck out all over
> the low hull, the greasy, slimy swell swung her up lazily and let
> her down, swaying her thin masts. In the empty immensity of
> earth, sky, and water, there she was, incomprehensible, firing
> into a continent. Pop, would go one of the six-inch guns; a small
> flame would dart and vanish, a little white smoke would disap-
> pear, a tiny projectile would give a feeble screech — and nothing
> happened. Nothing could happen. There was a touch of insanity

---

[12] Michel Foucault, *Madness and Civilization: A History of Insanity in the Age of
      Reason*, R. Howard (trans.), London: Tavistock, 1965. See also Roy Porter,
      Enlightenment: Britain and the Creation of the Modern World, London: Allen
      Lane, 2000, 215-218.

[13] Conrad's ellipsis. Conrad used ellipses relatively frequently in his letters
      and prose, and I have signalled when they appear in passages I have
      quoted. Ellipses that appear without such a signal are my conventional
      insertions to indicate where Conrad's original text has been edited.

> in the proceeding, a sense of lugubrious drollery in the sight; and
> it was not dissipated by somebody on board assuring me ear-
> nestly there was a camp of natives — he called them, enemies —
> hidden out of sight somewhere.[14]

This grotesquely pointless exercise is Marlow's introduction to
European-African relations, and surely says much about the sepa-
rateness of the two sets of cultures. How suggestive is this image of
the modern-day attempts of American soldiers, unschooled in Arab
custom, to stamp out the Iraqi insurgency, or indeed of any situation
where the writ of a government does not hold, whether in Somalia,
Southern Afghanistan, parts of Colombia, the housing projects of
America, British inner city estates or French *banlieues*. At the time of
writing, Britain's Royal Air Force has ordered £20 billionsworth of
Typhoon aircraft, while the Royal Navy is agitating to spend £3.6
billion on two aircraft carriers, while the principle threat to British
forces comes from AK-47s and improvised roadside bombs. The
opposition, for now, is not a massed army, nor does it hold territory;
the enemy can simply melt into the civilian population. One of
Conrad's great anticipations is the likely offensive response to
overwhelming force.

It is true that Conrad is uninterested in African or Malay culture;
his interests are in European politics, philosophy and the construction of psychological ideals at a time when, in Africa and elsewhere,
their shallowness was being exposed. The multiple ambiguities of
the title 'Heart of darkness' develop ideas of emptiness. Africa may
well be a dark continent, *terra incognita*, but there is nothing at the
centre of Kurtz, nothing of Leopold's philosophy other than a
Schwindel. However dark is the Congolese jungle, says Conrad, however primitive African civilisations, just take a look — if you dare —
inside Kurtz. It may not be politically correct to phrase things in that
way, but it is hard to see it as a statement about *Africans*. And it is
important not to forget that 'Heart of darkness' begins with Marlow
saying *London* has been "one of the dark places of the earth" and
ends not with the Congo but the *Thames* "seem[ing] to lead into the
heart of an immense darkness."

Conrad is certainly not interested in what postcolonial critics are
interested in, and they are entitled to point that out. But the use of
terms like 'racist' not only imposes our own values on someone writing a hundred years ago (and, moreover, someone writing a work of

---

[14]   The original manuscript piles on even more irony: in it the French were
       having one of their "heroic" wars.

fiction, not a political tract), but also assumes a crude model of psychological aetiology which is singularly inappropriate when applied to one of the more psychologically sophisticated writers in the canon. Achebe is absolutely right to claim that Africans do not have a voice in Conrad's work, and in 1975 that claim was probably more salutary than it may appear now. But he is wrong to suggest that Conrad was part of the conspiracy to deny them a voice. Conrad was simply not offering himself as a vehicle for such voices; that may mean that he is not a hero for the postcolonial theorists, but equally it does not make him a villain either. As Rino Zhuwarara argued, "writers such as Joseph Conrad can help start a debate about the fate of the oppressed, but, ultimately, they cannot be a substitute for the voices of the oppressed themselves." [15]

We can agree with the many commentators who have pointed out that Conrad "was a man of his times" (Singh's words) while still noting that he did a great deal to undermine the easy distinction between civilisation and savagery. Willems descends into savagery — Kurtz, worse, ascends into it. Conrad may or may not have been able to imagine what a world where the 'natives' were free of European domination would be like. He certainly chose not to imagine such a world, and surely novelists are not obliged to encompass every imaginative possibility. But with his deep opposition to the imperial enterprise, combined with a self-consciousness about his and his characters' involvement with it (a self-consciousness whose roots no doubt reach down to his and his family's experiences as members of a colonised nation), "he permits his later readers to imagine something other than an Africa carved up into dozens of European colonies, even if, for his own part, he had little notion of what that Africa might be", [16] to quote a fair-minded summary from Edward Said. [17]

---

[15] Rino Zhuwarara, '*Heart of Darkness* revisited: the African response', in Gene M. Moore (ed.), *Joseph Conrad's Heart of Darkness: A Casebook*, Oxford: Oxford University Press, 2004, 219-242, at 241.

[16] Edward W. Said, *Culture and Imperialism*, London: Chatto & Windus, 1993, 28.

[17] There are similar points to be made about the role of women in Conrad. Again, he had a tendency to underplay their problems, but this was largely due to his being interested in more 'male' themes. *Under Western Eyes* is perhaps his most interesting treatment of women, with its group of good and bad female characters in the Geneva scenes, and the appalling 'feminist' Peter Ivanovitch. 'Heart of darkness' is one story where he is very dismissive of women.

Globalisation and the end of history in Sulaco

Not all domination is military. Conrad was well aware of the subtler forms of control that the networked world offers. The late 19th century economy was highly interconnected, and as a seaman Conrad played a small part in that. Economic competition was not as untrammelled as nowadays; there were extreme free trade liberals around, but protectionism was generally assumed as an important political and financial tool for governments.

Nevertheless, the forces were still bracing. At the beginning of 'The end of the tether', the aging seaman Whalley strolls around Singapore, his world having been pushed aside by economic change. His days of glory, as a romantic, pioneering explorer (he has even had an island named after him) are over. In fact, it was the discoveries of himself and others, the foundation of trading relations with native populations, and the mapping of sea lanes (not to mention the opening of the Suez Canal), that have made the Eastern waters safe for the big trading companies, chiefly concerned with achieving economies of scale as they open up trade between Europe and the East. The ships have changed, risk is managed and the big companies play percentages. "The ships now had yellow funnels with black tops, and a time-table of appointed routes like a confounded service of tramways. The winds of December and June were all one to them." Sailing has become a job, not a vocation. As Said puts it, "the business of empire, once an adventurous and often individualistic enterprise, had become the empire of business."[18] In this newly pragmatic context, it is appropriate that Marlow should tell the story of the expedition to find Kurtz to an audience of businessmen. Captain Whalley is respected in this new world, but his day is gone.

In Conrad's most ambitious book *Nostromo*, the nature of the new world dominated by "material interests", very familiar to us, is explored in some depth. Costaguana is a small independent South American republic, which has toiled under a series of revolutions and incompetent, venal governments for years. The novel begins with Charles Gould, a native Costaguanan of English descent, returning from exile to take up his inheritance of the San Tomé silver mine, near Sulaco, a provincial capital. The mine is a potential source of vast wealth, but of great pain to Gould's father; successive governments have driven Gould Sr. to despair and death by their excessive demands for taxation and rent, taxing the silver even before it had

---

[18]   Said, *Culture and Imperialism*, 25.

left the ground. Long-term investment in the mine had never been considered, and each government exploited it for short-term gain; the result, as any economist would warn, was that the mine had gone out of business.

Charles Gould, however, decides to make the mine work, hoping that the success of a well-run enterprise would make the politics of Costaguana more rational, by showing how stability and sensible, long-term decisions produce benefits for all. As Gould explains it:

> What is wanted here is law, good faith, order, security. Anyone can declaim about these things, but I pin my faith to material interests. Only let the material interests once get a firm footing, and they are bound to impose the conditions on which alone they can continue to exist. That's how your money-making is justified here in the face of lawlessness and disorder. It is justified because the security which it demands must be shared with an oppressed people. A better justice will come afterwards. That's your ray of hope.

So "the authorities of Sulaco had learned that the San Tomé mine could make it worth their while to leave things and people alone." The newly-operational mine gradually starts to produce output, and foreign developers move in, increasing productivity by installing transport infrastructure. Mr Holroyd, a shadowy American financier, nurtures the mine from a distance. But ultimately, Gould must take a gamble—he lets go his political neutrality, and becomes an active supporter of the liberal presidency of Don Vincente Ribiera. The reader has already been told in Chapter Two of *Nostromo* that Ribiera's government falls after a *coup* by the head of the armed forces and his brutish brother, and that Ribiera himself had made a humiliating retreat from a lost battle on a lame mule.

Gould's response is to send the extant mined silver by ship to Europe, but the plan fails, and instead the silver has to be hidden; only a single man, Nostromo, knows its whereabouts. He, the self-styled 'Capataz de Cargadores' (Captain of the Dockers) who has long lived on his reputation as a legendary figure, capable of the most audacious feats of endurance and heroism, returns to Sulaco and performs his last marvellous action, an historic journey to summon a loyal general to relieve the siege of Sulaco and defeat the *coup*. But he doesn't disabuse anyone of the notion that the silver has been lost, and instead lives on the buried treasure. His life is now comfortable, and the esteem in which he is held is higher than ever, but the duplicities upon which they are based undermine him; he is killed, farcically, as a result of a mistaken identity — ironically, he is mistaken for a thief, although a thief is precisely what he is.

The tale appears to be a boost for the material interests, and to some extent it is, as it seems obvious to this reader at least that the law and order fostered by the mine is preferable to the "lawlessness and disorder" of the previous regime of Guzman Bento or the likely government of the *coup*-leader Montero. The parallels with some events in present-day South America are surprisingly strong. The populist government of Evo Morales, Bolivia's first indigenous President, has promoted the nationalisation of hydrocarbon resources, partly as a nationalistic gesture of expropriation of control of what are seen as national assets from foreign 'material interests' (which as a matter of fact are mainly Brazilian), and partly to redress the balance of overly-generous exploitation contracts drawn up during a period of low oil and gas prices.

But there is another side to the Bolivian story. The state hydrocarbon company YPFB had reduced known gas reserves to pretty close to zero by the mid-1990s, had been deprived of investment capital, and had no money to look for more. The value of the gas assets (and YPFB accounted for 9% of Bolivia's GDP in 1994) was dwindling, and the neo-liberal government of the day privatised the giant corporation. Within a couple of years of that controversial move, the explorations of various private, largely foreign-owned consortia revealed that the actual size of Bolivia's gas reserves was 600% higher than previously thought. Without foreign investment in the mid-to-late 90s, the gas that powered the Morales victory would have remained hidden underground. This triumph of popular democracy needed international capital to fund it; the irony, which Conrad would certainly have appreciated, is that popular discontent at the exploitation by foreigners of Bolivian assets would never had arisen if the foreigners had not discovered the assets themselves. Left to their own devices, the Bolivians were never prepared, for whatever reason, to invest sufficient money into YPFB's exploration efforts.

Similarly, Argentina's government had run up a large amount of debt during the 1990s, partly thanks to a then-popular decision to peg the peso to the US dollar. This helped tame the horrendous inflation that caused so much misery, but as the government did not rein in its spending, the result was an escalation of debt. The fixed exchange rate made imports cheap, and money leaked out of the country; either devaluation or a reduction of public spending (and of the waste of public money through corruption and tax evasion) were needed, but neither happened. People, quite rationally, would buy underpriced US dollars with their pesos, and invest abroad. Eventually a debt crisis claimed a succession of Argentine governments, and only drastic action, a debt default, saved the day. The Argentine economy is slowly recovering, but at a cost — Argentina is not seen as a very good investment nowadays, and an authoritarian strain of government has been encouraged.

In many countries, there are curious situations whereby a bad situation is created by incompetent or corrupt, often populist governments, which is partially resolved by outside intervention by wealthy foreigners. Such intervention usually has strings attached (even foreign aid and interventions by NGOs are conditional nowadays). But when those strings are pulled, anti-foreigner populism is almost irresistible because of the manifest unfairness of a nation's people paying the price for the profligacy of its governments. Indeed, it was precisely such a populist appeal that led to the attempted *coup* in *Nostromo*: "The Minister of War, in a barrack-square allocution to the officers of the artillery regiment he had been inspecting, had declared the national honour sold to foreigners. The Dictator, by his weak compliance with the demands of the European powers — for the settlement of long outstanding money claims — had shown himself unfit to rule." Foreign material interests are usually unable to influence media or political presentation of the situation, and it is in the interests of political elites to underplay the role that previous governments have played.

We can put a proxy figure on the difficulties of foreign firms via the insurance market. The Berne Union, the leading international organisation for the export credit and investment insurance industry, reports that its members wrote more than $44 *billion* in coverage for protection for companies against political risks in 2006, up from $37 billion in 2005 — not a small amount of money that firms collectively feel they need to put aside.

In a masterly piece of political theory, Francis Fukuyama once looked forward to the 'end of history'.[19] Fukuyama, on the fringe of neo-conservative thinking in Washington, is usually wrong in his answers to questions, but is brilliant at spotting the questions to ask. After the triumph of the international coalition assembled by George Bush Sr. under the auspices of the UN in 1990, shortly after the igno-

---

[19]   Francis Fukuyama, *The End of History and the Last Man*, New York: Free Press, 1992.

minious collapse of the Soviet Union and the removal of any kind of figleaf of credibility from Marxist theory, Fukuyama announced that history, in the sense of giant clashes of ideology, had ended, and that we had seen something like the triumph of liberalism, democracy and capitalism.

Of course, from the standpoint of 2007, this looks like ludicrous stuff; even by Fukuyama's standards he was spectacularly wrong. The ideology of Islamism has spread across the globe, sometimes in virulent and appallingly violent form. The anti-globalisation and anti-capitalism movements, intellectually as incoherent as you can get, have a powerful hold even in the universities of the Western democracies where you would hope a more critical attitude would prevail (a Conradian irony: university lecturers, whose stipends depend on the surpluses produced by capitalism, denounce capitalism without fear of political oppression, while being paid by the very governments they hope to deconstruct!). Hugo Chávez, the Venezuelan strongman, rails against the United States, looking every inch the populist oil-fuelled *caudillo*, and is lauded as a super-democrat even as he rules by decree and shuts down opposition-supporting television stations. Meanwhile our increasing understanding of climate change and environmental degradation lends support to ecologist ideologies and undermines the claims of liberalism to distribute resources most fairly and effectively.

So Fukuyama's analysis does not hold water. To be fair that was less obvious when he wrote it. Even Edward Said seemed to accept the truth, if not the desirability, of Fukuyama's theory,[20] while "mine is the first generation able to contemplate the possibility that we may live our entire lives without going to war or sending our children to war," said Tony Blair (of all people) in 1997. But the question Fukuyama asks—why should anyone *not* prefer liberal democracy and capitalism, which provide precisely the stability, fairness and prosperity that Charles Gould looks forward to?—is an extremely good one, because in effect the events of the 21st century so far have shown that there are many people who would rather follow other ideologies, religions, faiths or creeds than live in a stable, fair or prosperous world. And it is not entirely clear why this should be. *The Secret Agent* gives a cynical and ironic explanation.

> For obviously one does not revolt against the advantages and opportunities of that state, but against the price which must be

---

[20]   Said, *Culture and Imperialism*, 313.

paid for the same in the coin of accepted morality, self-restraint and toil.

In *Victory*, thuggish Martin Ricardo gives another defence of a degenerate human dignity.

> I follow a gentleman. That ain't the same thing as to serve an employer. They give you wages as they'd fling a bone to a dog, and they expect you to be grateful. It's worse than slavery. You don't expect a slave that's bought for money to be grateful. And if you sell your work — what is it but selling your own self?

The worst thing that Ricardo can conceive is being "tame". He is an extreme character, but ultimately he speaks for all those who wish to control their own destinies. In *Nostromo*, Gould argues pragmatically with Montero that he will not give over the mine to the revolutionaries. He finds it embarrassing to talk in terms of abstract justice, but ultimately it is the part that the mine plays in the Costaguanan economy, and in paying its politicians, that hits home. What this ultimately means is that it is the material interests behind the silver mine that dictate what Costaguanan policy is to be. This may objectively be a good thing for Costaguana, but it removes a level of autonomy from the nation. Politics and human interests are often subjective, and the result is awkwardly akin to imperialism (a particular problem for American neo-conservative analysts who, mindful of 1776, abhor empire). But we see how close the material interests are to an imperial position when Conrad tells us of the financier Holroyd's "imaginative satisfaction" in running Costaguana from afar through its silver mine, even if "in this aberration of his genius he served the progress of the world."

As *Nostromo* develops, the material interests win their battles and the Occidental Province, which contains the mine and of which Sulaco is the capital, secedes from Costaguana. It enters its modern period under President Lopez, supported by Gould and his silver concession, but all is not well. The prosperity predicted by Gould occurs, while Costaguana remains poor and its politics immature; the inequalities make some wish to reunite the country. Gould wished to depoliticise the distribution of resources and the pursuit of prosperity, but he gradually realises that material interest is only one of the interests at large in a nation.

> He might have known ... that Ribierism could never come to anything. The mine had corrupted his judgement by making him sick of bribing and intriguing merely to have his work left alone from day to day. Like his father, he did not like to be robbed. It

exasperated him. He had persuaded himself that, apart from higher considerations, the backing up of Don José's hopes of reform was good business. He had gone forth into the senseless fray as his poor uncle, whose sword hung on the wall of his study, had gone forth — in the defence of the commonest decencies of organized society. Only his weapon was the wealth of the mine, more far-reaching and subtle than an honest blade of steel fitted into a simple brass guard.

More dangerous to the wielder, too, this weapon of wealth, double-edged with the cupidity and misery of mankind, steeped in all the vices of self-indulgence as in a concoction of poisonous roots, tainting the very cause for which it is drawn, always ready to turn awkwardly in the hand. There was nothing for it now but to go on using it. But he promised himself to see it shattered into small bits before he let it be wrenched from his grasp.

Or, as the engineer-in-chief of the rail link to the mine puts it:

The tale of killing the goose with the golden eggs has not been evolved for nothing out of the wisdom of mankind. It is a story that will never grow old. That is why Charles Gould in his deep, dumb way has countenanced the Ribierist Mandate, the first public act that promised him safety on other than venal grounds. Ribierism has failed, as everything merely rational fails in this country.

The mine cannot be an instrument of abstract justice, or any other principle, as its power does not stem from "methods of probity" or "the sense of usefulness". As the cynical Dr Monygham (often taken as Conrad's spokesman) points out, "The Gould concession had ransomed its way through all those years." The foundation of its power is, ultimately, the greed of those with interests in it. Like the idealism behind imperialism, material interests cannot support the laudable social aims of a Gould (or a Fukuyama). "And now the mine was back again in its old path, with the disadvantage that henceforth it had to deal not only with the greed provoked by its wealth, but with the resentment awakened by the attempt to free itself from its bondage to moral corruption." As the crisis recedes, Monygham can see more trouble in the future.

There is no peace and no rest in the development of material interests. They have their law, and their justice. But it is founded on expediency, and is inhuman: it is without rectitude, without the continuity and the force that can be found only in a moral principle. Mrs Gould, the time approaches when all that the Gould concession stands for shall weigh as heavily upon the people as the barbarism, cruelty, and misrule of a few years back.

Democracy is not a way out, because it, possibly for historically contingent reasons, has become closely tied with those very material interests which weigh the people down — here Conrad agrees with Fukuyama and the neo-cons, who of course have a much more positive view of democracy and capitalism. Conrad makes this argument explicitly in the essay 'Autocracy and war'.

> Industrialism and commercialism — wearing high-sounding names in many languages (*Welt-politik* may serve for one instance) picking up coins behind the severe and disdainful figure of science whose giant strides have widened for us the horizon of the universe by some few inches — stand ready, almost eager, to appeal to the sword as soon as the globe of the earth has shrunk beneath our growing numbers by another ell or so. And democracy, which has elected to pin its faith to the supremacy of material interests, will have to fight their battles to the bitter end, on a mere pittance — unless, indeed, some statesman of exceptional ability and overwhelming prestige succeeds in carrying through an international understanding for the delimitation of spheres of trade all over the earth ... .

At the end of the novel, in the eyes of the compassionate Mrs Gould (an Englishwoman), the San Tomé mountain hangs "over the whole land, feared, hated, wealthy; more soulless than any tyrant, more pitiless and autocratic than the worst Government; ready to crush innumerable lives in the expansion of its greatness." The "ideal perfection of confidence" — a nice ironic phrase for us to recall following the decline of the neo-conservative view of the world[21] — cannot legitimately create conditions of rationality and perfection, especially in a nation whose politics are frankly immature. A push to modernity merely provides modern tools for pre-modern groups to pursue their ideals, however barbarous. Conrad's view of international politics, pessimistic and conservative as it no doubt is, is as topical now as it was in 1904.

---

[21]   Which Fukuyama has described very effectively. Francis Fukuyama, *After the Neocons: America at the Crossroads*, London: Profile Books, 2006.

Chapter Three

Guilt and Pity

Guilt

The colonial enterprise was responsible for a lot of wrongs, including the coercion of colonial populations, the gradual corruption visited on undeveloped populations by the import of a new set of values, and the exacerbation of immature and violent politics by providing avenues for greed and excuses for rebellion. Conrad's main geopolitical interest is with European culture and thought, and the effects on *that* culture of being, and having been, illegitimate colonisers, and in that context one immediate response, a very personal and self-centred one, to one's own destruction of the health, prosperity, character, independence or hopes of others, is guilt. A number of Conrad's finest creations are driven by guilt, notably Razumov in *Under Western Eyes* and Jim in *Lord Jim*. Jim is a "simple" young man, the son of an English parson, entranced by the heroic and moral life of the coloniser who becomes a seaman in the East. But when his ship, the *Patna* (on which he is first mate), strikes a submerged object, the white members of the crew, including the Captain, decide to abandon ship and take to the lifeboats — despite the fact that the 'cargo' is a group of 800 pilgrims bound for Mecca from Singapore. Initially, Jim tries to dissociate himself from the contemptible action, although he doesn't try to prevent it; there is nothing he can do. But when another crew member collapses, he impulsively jumps into the lifeboat and takes his place *incognito*, acutely conscious of having left the pilgrims to die (the accident is at night — most of them will drown in their sleep).

But the situation is not as bad as the crew has feared, and the ship does *not* sink — instead it is intercepted by a French gunboat while drifting. The facts are pretty clear, and there is an official inquiry, during which the Captain and the rest of the crew abscond, but Jim stays to face the music, and loses his mariner's certificate. The disgrace is public and disciplinary, but at the same time personal — he has betrayed all the ideals that he has held dear.

The tale shows Jim from the outside, as Conrad's ambiguous narrator Marlow tries to find lessons from his search for redemption. Marlow pieces together the story of Jim's travels as he attempts to efface his identity and accommodate his guilt. Working onshore as a chandler's clerk, he stays at each new port only as long as he remains unrecognised; slowly he moves Eastwards, pursued by gossip. Eventually, he becomes manager of a trading post in Sumatra, where he helps the elderly rajah defeat powerful enemies, and becomes an important part of the community. Finally he is able to apply the imperial ideals that took him to sea in the first place. He becomes known, in the Malay language, as "Lord Jim". But he loses his honour once more when the tropical paradise is invaded by a gang of cutthroats. He has the chance to kill the gang, but humanely agrees to escort them to safety; they kill the rajah's son in the course of their leaving. Jim once more must face a society whose morals he has outraged; he surrenders himself to the rajah, who shoots him dead.

Razumov is similarly tortured in *Under Western Eyes*. He is a conservative student in Russia, with no family and precious few friends. His life is irrevocably changed when an idealistic fellow student Haldin assassinates a senior government minister, and, knowing Razumov slightly and respecting him, tries to enlist his help in escape. Razumov is horrified, partly at the violence he is expected to condone ("A murder is a murder"), and partly because of the risk to his ambitions. Haldin has assumed that Razumov's serious and intellectual demeanour make him a revolutionary, with the unspoken premise that only the brutish, or stupid, or those who benefit from the status quo could possibly support what the author himself called "the ferocity and imbecility of an autocratic rule rejecting all legality and in fact basing itself upon complete moral anarchism."[1] Razumov is dumbfounded by Haldin's confidences; he initially tries to help, but is thwarted when a vital contact is discovered dead drunk. Horrified by the prospect of having to keep Haldin concealed for longer, Razumov betrays him to the authorities. The strain of these events is palpable in Part I of the novel, whose charged atmosphere is rendered brilliantly with Dostoyevskyan verve — ironic as Conrad insisted he disliked Dostoyevsky intensely. But Razumov — the name is derived from the Russian word for 'reason' — reads very

---

[1]   In the 'Author's note' to *Under Western Eyes*.

much like an anti-Raskolnikov, a man forced to be audacious and decisive against his will. His rationalisations are hollow.

> Betray. A great word. What is betrayal? They talk of a man betraying his country, his friends, his sweetheart. There must be a moral bond first. All a man can betray is his conscience. And how is my conscience engaged here; by what bond of common faith, of common conviction, am I obliged to let that fanatical idiot drag me down with him? On the contrary — every obligation of true courage is the other way.

He cannot convince himself this is so. His first attempt at expiating the guilt he knows is lodged within him is a characteristically intellectual one: he tries to reassert consistency in his life by becoming a police spy and infiltrating the exiled revolutionary organisation in Geneva and elsewhere. But there is neither consistency nor redemption here. In the course of his new career he meets, and falls in love with, Haldin's sister. He is not fully trusted by the revolutionaries until they receive intelligence from Russia that they incorrectly interpret as exonerating him. Now he is free of any possibility of exposure, he confesses his guilt to the sister, and then to the revolutionaries. He is attacked, mutilated and crippled.

Guilt is not something that can be thrown off, either by flight (Jim) or cynicism (Razumov). Once it has been accrued, it is a burden, and this is insufficiently appreciated in many political contexts. History may be constantly reinterpreted, but it doesn't go away, and reactions of enmity or guilt cannot be swept aside even by the most generous accommodation. Redemption cannot be whistled up like the wind, or imposed on oneself. At the close of Part I of *Under Western Eyes*, Razumov, being interviewed by Councillor Mikulin of the secret police, tries to force an end to his predicament, one way or the other.

> 'What is all this mockery? Of course, you can send me straight from this room to Siberia. That would be intelligible. To what is intelligible I can submit. But I protest against this comedy of persecution. ... But, really, I must claim the right to be done once for all with [Haldin]. And in order to accomplish this I shall take the liberty ...'
>
> Razumov on his side of the table bowed slightly to the seated bureaucrat.
>
> '... To retire — simply to retire,' he finished with great resolution.

He walked to the door, thinking, 'Now he must show his hand. He must ring and have me arrested before I am out of the building, or he must let me go. And either way ...'

An unhurried voice said —

'Kirylo Sidorovitch.' [i.e. Razumov's patronymic name]

Razumov at the door turned his head.

'To retire,' he repeated.

'Where to?' asked Councillor Mikulin softly.

Mikulin's naïve, even conversational question contains and conceals deadly force, because Razumov *cannot* retire after the betrayal. His refusal to help Haldin condemned him to a radical narrowing of choice and control. More irony, and a terrible fate; after all, it was in order *not* to be drawn into a particular life that he betrayed Haldin in the first place. Circumstances had to bind Razumov for or against the revolutionaries, within or without the secret police. Confronting the revolutionary forces, whether facing or opposing them, became a simple irresistible imperative. There is no way through the antagonisms.

Redemption cannot be taken off the shelf. An act in bad faith, or in ignorance, or in haste remains forever. An act of some importance changes the world, and cannot be wished away. Jim and Razumov find that submitting to the rough justice of a swift and violent accounting is the end point of their long journeys. They command compassion, despite the wrongs that placed them where they are. But in the context of wrongs committed, Conrad tells us that guilt cannot make a significant difference. There is nowhere to retire. Isolationism, in a complex world with a history of unfortunate interaction, is not an option.

Pity

If we can't expiate moral failure by looking inward, then the alternative is to look outward, attempting some kind of sympathy for the victim — the result is pity, and Conrad was deeply sceptical about the value of that as well. That is not to say, as some commentators have suggested, that Conrad was an early adopter of a hard-nosed Nietzschean philosophy of radical scepticism about morality and compassion *per se*,[2] although he clearly was interested in Nietzsche's

---

[2]   Cf. e.g. Daphna Erdinast-Vulcan, *Joseph Conrad and the Modern Temper*, Oxford: Clarendon Press, 1991, where she argues that Conrad's characters

ideas which get an airing in a number of places. For instance, in *Victory*, Heyst's father is a quasi-Nietzschean philosopher, perpetually berating an uninterested public, and "claim[ing] for mankind that right to absolute moral and intellectual liberty of which he no longer believed them worthy." Heyst Sr. tells his son, on his deathbed, that pity is nothing more than a form of contempt, the least difficult type of contempt to hold, but also a hypocritical one, as "you, too, if you are anything, are as pitiful as the rest." Pity is not effective; towards the end of *Nostromo* as Gould's dreams for the Occidental Republic unravel, Mrs Gould lies down in her beautiful garden, "resembl[ing] a good fairy, weary of a long career of well-doing, touched by the withering suspicion of the uselessness of her labours, the powerlessness of her magic."

The Nigger of the "Narcissus" is the story of a ship as it sails home to London from Bombay. The crew is tight-knit and disciplined under the efficient Captain Allistoun, but the stability of the unit is threatened by two new members. Donkin, a destitute Cockney, is an insubordinate rabble-rouser, but the very late arrival James Wait (the eponymous 'nigger') is more of a threat. Soon after the ship has sailed, Wait develops symptoms of illness which render him bedridden. The crew are diverted from their duties by their efforts to take care of Wait, and obey his every whim like "base courtiers." But Wait is never grateful, and each attempt to please is met by further surliness. When he complains about the food, one sailor steals an officer's meal for him, but Wait is ungracious; a fight breaks out, which ends with Wait's coughing fit. When the forecastle floods, Wait berates his heroic rescuers for their delay. One sailor goes cold because he has put his coat over Wait to keep him warm; Wait complains about being unable to breathe. The crew speculate throughout as to whether Wait is malingering, but they, with the exception of Donkin, cannot bring themselves to confront him openly. Donkin meanwhile continues to goad authority, and loses a front tooth to the first mate for his pains, but the Captain's leadership just about holds. Difficult conditions pull the crew back together as a team, and Donkin's rebellion is seen for what it is, a refusal to pull his weight.

Wait finally admits feigning illness to Donkin in the privacy of the sick bay. But he is declining anyway, terrified by the thought of death, and by an attempt by one evangelical crew member to save his soul. He tries to recover himself by recommencing work, but the

are in perpetually active revolt against the 'modern temper' of radical Nietzschean scepticism—revolts that ultimately fail.

Captain refuses, accusing him of faking. A superstition begins to spread through the crew that Wait will die at the sight of land, and indeed he does, as he tries to prevent Donkin from robbing him. The loss of Wait, though it removes an impediment to the crew's unity, in fact deprives them of the "respectable bond of a sentimental lie." But although Wait's body almost refuses to be buried at sea, when he finally leaves the ship a fair breeze appears, and takes them back to an idealistically-rendered England. The crew reject Donkin, and say their goodbyes at a pub, but the narrator of the story never sees them again.

The writings and sayings of Heyst Sr. in *Victory* express the Nietzchean idea that the man who rejects conventional ('slave') morality is necessarily pitiless. On board the *Narcissus*, we see the converse effect: the sensitivity of the crew to Wait's plight hinders their unity, discipline and ability to sail the ship. Pity is one aspect of the social glue that keeps society together, of course; to an extent Wait would have earned (and the crew tacitly takes him to have earned) their pity as a result of the solidarity that makes the crew a crew, as opposed to a disparate group of men who happen to be engaged on a common enterprise. But we know that Wait was not deserving.

The older sailor Singleton, "a lonely relic of a devoured and forgotten generation", seems unusually devoid of humanitarian concern for Wait, as if alive to the extraneousness of a single individual in the face of a task requiring not just collaboration but a 'culture' to sustain it. We cannot ignore individuals' problems, but neither can we deal with each case of misfortune individually. The resources that we would need to expend are simply too high, the chances of success too low, our understanding of others' needs too limited, and the effects on social connectivity too radical. And deep down, action driven by pity assumes that the recipient is a victim pure and simple, has not contributed to his or her downfall, indeed is not a social actor in any meaningful sense. Pity has a strong link with contempt, as Heyst Sr asserts, and as Conrad the author strongly implies, in the 'Author's note' to *The Secret Agent*. In that novel, the simpleton Stevie has boundless compassion for the poor and oppressed, and this is to the young man's credit. But that is hardly sustainable as an account of how to run the world; there is no practical suggestion of how to foster or sustain the social institutions to minimise the total unhappiness of mankind. Certainly Stevie's compassion lacks any kind of implementation strategy, and often expresses itself violently, for instance when he lets off a series of fireworks on the staircase in the office in which he works. Pity leads to anger, and cannot support political action. Eschewing moral complexity is too flawed a way to judge the issues. This is where the revolutionaries go wrong, such as the reasonable but misguided Sophia Antonovna in *Under Western Eyes*, one of Conrad's sympathetic portraits of a revolutionary.

> Truly there are millions of people in Russia who would envy the life of dogs in this country [Switzerland]. It is a horror and a shame to confess this even between ourselves. One must believe for very pity. This can't go on. No! It can't go on. For twenty years I have been coming and going, looking neither to the left nor to the right ... What are you [i.e., Razumov, posing as a revolutionary, to whom she is speaking] smiling to yourself for? You are only at the beginning. You have begun well, but you just wait till you have trodden every particle of yourself under your feet in your comings and goings. For that is what it comes to. You've got to trample down every particle of your own feelings; for stop you cannot, you must not.[3]

Sophia's sympathy is deep, but in the end she is dehumanising herself, not only through her revolutionary work, but also by devoting herself to Peter Ivanovitch's anarchist theories. Change brought about by inhuman agents cannot lead to a moral society.

In a perceptive essay, Michael Ignatieff[4] has written of the growing influence of the news media in the world of politics. Guilt and pity are both conjured up by pictures of famine, war, repression and disease shown on our TV screens each night. Such pictures abstract essentially from context and history, and conceal as much as they reveal — which is not to underplay the significance of the revelations. Ignatieff wrote about the upheaval following the collapse of Yugoslavia, a traumatic event, but news footage contained few indications of the complex history, with its several interpretations, that preceded it. Similar examples could be cited nowadays. News pictures from Zimbabwe reveal the ghastly nature of Robert Mugabe's degenerating regime, and quite right too, but downplay many of the positive aspects of Mugabe's rule, such as his genuine commitment to education. Britain's failure to follow through on promises made at independence to manage the transfer of land from wealthy white landowners to landless peasants is a factor that is absent from the TV

---

[3]   Conrad's ellipsis.
[4]   Michael Ignatieff, 'Is nothing sacred? The ethics of television', in *The Warrior's Honor: Ethnic War and the Modern Conscience*, London: Chatto & Windus, 1998, 9-33.

pictures and also seems unimportant when viewing footage of Morgan Tsvangirai, the Zimbabwean opposition leader, with a swollen eye and broken skull after a beating by Mugabe's thugs. The story is a complex one, which in some way accounts for the reluctance of African leaders to criticise Mugabe (despite British and American urging). But the TV screens continue to show the decontextualised horror.

Ignatieff's point is that, in a democracy, these images count. In a democracy, wrote Conrad, leadership was "without other ancestry but the sudden shout of a multitude,"[5] and Ignatieff argues that the TV news has an enormous influence on what is shouted. 'Something must be done', is the cry, and wars start and interventions are made on the back of compassionate thoughts, driven by pity certainly, guilt sometimes. Rational argument cannot make its way in the world of disconnected images of undoubted suffering. As Conrad warns in the essay 'Autocracy and war', "The printed page of the Press makes a sort of still uproar, taking from men both the power to reflect and the faculty of genuine feeling; leaving them only the artificially created need of having something exciting to talk about." Guilt and pity force their way into our politics; these private, subjective theses drive policy (not only foreign policy) and reduce the public space for reflection, argument and realism.[6]

Images go beyond the press with their immediacy.

> An overworked horse falling in front of our windows, a man writhing under a cart-wheel in the street, awaken more genuine emotion, more horror, pity, and indignation than the stream of reports, appalling in their monotony, of tens of thousands of decaying bodies tainting the air of the Manchurian plains, of other tens of thousands of maimed bodies groaning in ditches, crawling on the frozen ground, filling the field hospitals; of the hundreds of thousands of survivors no less pathetic and even more tragic in being left alive by fate to the wretched exhaustion of their pitiful toil.

The facts, the context, the assessed extent of the disaster have less impact than the image. Our pity is irrational, manipulable.

> In this age of knowledge our sympathetic imagination, to which alone we can look for the ultimate triumph of concord and justice, remains strangely impervious to information, however correctly and even picturesquely conveyed. As to the vaunted

---

[5] From 'Autocracy and war'.
[6] Richard Sennett, *The Fall of Public Man*, New York: Alfred A. Knopf, Inc, 1977.

eloquence of a serried array of figures, it has all the futility of precision without force. It is the exploded superstition of enthusiastic statisticians.

The TV news aligns individual propensities for demanding action
based on guilt or pity, and turns those worries into a social force,
very much as Wait's plight aligns the sensitivities of the crew of the
Narcissus. But on the *Narcissus*, Capt. Allistoun heads a hierarchy
that (once the problem of insubordination is dealt with) still func-
tions as a problem-solving structure; in a democracy, the more nebulous forces of guilt and pity demand action, and punish inaction,
without seriously tackling (or even diagnosing) underlying problems.

So, for instance, a great deal of laudable public sentiment supports
drives to make poverty history, and increase aid. Ever since the
remarkable success of Band Aid, people have shown their compassion and willingness to make tangible contributions. But two
decades on, poverty still persists. The blame for this is directed at
'others' — governments, the World Bank, multinationals. But
well-meaning individuals like Bono or Bob Geldof, who have tire-
lessly campaigned for aid for the developing world, are not account-
able for their actions, and would never think of resigning despite
their lack of success.[7] The hard questions — how to tackle the causes
of slow growth endemic in parts of the developing world, including
corruption, war, suppression of women's rights, lack of press freedom, and unconstructive politics — are not, and cannot be, tackled
by annual orgies of gift-giving.

---

[7]   William Easterly, *The White Man's Burden: Why the West's Efforts to Aid the
       Rest Have Done So Much Ill and So Little Good*, New York: Penguin Press, 2006,
       15-17, 171-173, 369-371.

Chapter Four

The Urge to Revolt

Rebellion

If pity and guilt are inadequate as reactions to wrongs done, and inactivity is not a serious option once one is confronted by the antagonisms of the day, then action seems inevitable. And one very understandable urge is to change or break the system that creates wrongs — the revolutionary urge.

This was certainly an urge that Conrad knew, as a direct result of his unhappy early days. The premature death of his mother as an indirect result of his father's revolutionary activities was obviously hard, and in a late story, 'Prince Roman', he fuses the loss of a loved one with the loss of independence; the Prince, newly bereaved, goes to fight the Russians in the 1830–1 uprising with the words "I go where something louder than my grief and yet something with a voice very like it calls me." The premature deaths of Conrad's parents would also have driven home the potential for futile expenditure of valuable energy and life in a lost cause. His Uncle Tadeusz will have provided another model of caution and stability underpinning his love. It was an ambiguous inheritance.

Politically, Poland was under the Russian yoke, and Conrad bowed to no-one in his detestation of Russian politics — *Under Western Eyes* expresses the powerful urge to resist in the shadow of Russian autocracy, and the long harangue of the essay 'Autocracy and war', written shortly after *Nostromo*, is a powerful blast against Russia and its "evil counsellor" Prussia, demanding "the verdict that the Russia of today has not the right to give her voice on a single question touching the future of humanity, because from the very inception of her being the brutal destruction of dignity, of truth, of rectitude, of all that is faithful in human nature has been made the imperative condition of her existence." The Russian ruler when Conrad wrote was Tsar Nicholas II, but he might equally have been writing of Lenin or Stalin, of the ghastly bureaucrat Brezhnev, or the brutal and arbitrary Vladimir Putin. Conrad was prescient to see the essential irrationality of Russian autocracy necessitating its eventual collapse. But he would have been horrified to see the Russians, with a foreign policy still essentially nationalistic and based on a zero-sum model, sitting as a permanent member, with a veto, on the Security Council of the United Nations.

The 'Author's note' to *A Personal Record* talks of the simple urge to throw off this awful deadening hand; Poland, he argues, has a mentality that is "Western in complexion" and "even in religious matters, in sympathy with the most liberal currents of European thought." But this yearning for freedom was not, strictly speaking, revolutionary.

> One of the most sympathetic of my critics tried to account for certain characteristics of my work by the fact of my being, in his own words, "the son of a Revolutionist." No epithet could be more inapplicable to a man with such a strong sense of responsibility in the region of ideas and action and so indifferent to the promptings of personal ambition as my father. Why the description "revolutionary" should have been applied all through Europe to the Polish risings of 1831 and 1863 I really cannot understand. These risings were purely revolts against foreign domination. The Russians themselves called them "rebellions," which, from their point of view, was the exact truth. Amongst the men concerned in the preliminaries of the 1863 movement my father was no more revolutionary than the others, in the sense of working for the subversion of any social or political scheme of existence. He was simply a patriot in the sense of a man who believing in the spirituality of a national existence could not bear to see that spirit enslaved.

Conrad writes as if the simple non-revolutionary rebellion against the Russians would restore the balance. This may have been so — when Poland achieved total independence from the Soviet Union and the communist ideology, it did move Westward politically and eventually joined the European Union. But suspicion of Germany still prevails, and it is an awkward customer, struggling to come to terms with its communist past (for instance, attempts to uproot the network of contacts and spies from the communist era poison Polish politics even in 2007).

But occupations and "material interests" do change things. Imperialism in Africa did not simply occupy African territory, it hoped to change Africans (Conrad uses a cruder term) into "buying machine[s]". Throwing off a colonial ruler is not always trivial, as the colonial experience changes so much. And a liberation struggle can often seem, to those taking part in it, to entail the destruction of existing institutions and structures, as Conrad remarked in the 'Author's note' to *Under Western Eyes*.

> The most terrifying reflection (I am speaking now for myself) is that all these [characters in the novel] are not the product of the exceptional but of the general — of the normality of their place, and time, and race. The ferocity and imbecility of an autocratic rule rejecting all legality and in fact basing itself upon complete moral anarchism provokes the no less imbecile and atrocious answer of a purely Utopian revolutionism encompassing destruction by the first means to hand, in the strange conviction that a fundamental change of hearts must follow the downfall of any given human institutions.

In 'Prince Roman' there is clearly a wrestling match within the author himself, as he struggles to square his anti-revolutionary conservatism with his romantic love for his oppressed motherland. While the Prince goes to fight the Russian overlords, his father, "moved and uneasy, speaking from a purely aristocratic point of view, mistrusted the popular origins of the movement, regretted its democratic tendencies, and did not believe in the possibility of success." He worries about the "secular principles of legitimacy and order which have been violated in this reckless enterprise for the sake of most subversive illusions." But ultimately, Conrad's portrayal of Prince John is as a timid, political man, perhaps appropriately a Polonius figure, and it is Prince Roman's honour, love of country and fidelity to the cause that earn the author's approbation. This is perhaps a posthumous victory for his father Apollo over his Uncle Tadeusz. But even when the cause is so dear to his heart, Conrad finds it hard to allow the revolutionary voice to be heard unquestioned.

Violent revolution was an important part of political life in Conrad's day, as it is in ours. But why should Utopia be so imbecilic and atrocious?

Intellectualising revolt

The early part of Conrad's life was a time of globalised revolt. He was born only nine years after the revolutionary year of 1848, and anarchism and socialism, as well as various nationalist movements, were powerful ideologies which had sprouted violent wings. The caricature of the anarchist, with dark hat and beard, carrying a bomb (with a fizzing fuse and 'BOMB' written on it) was a comic representation of a very real threat. Hundreds of people died at the hands of terrorists between 1880 and the First World War; leaders assassinated by anarchists included Empress Elizabeth of Austria, King Umberto of Italy, Presidents Carnot of France and McKinley of the USA and Prime Ministers Antonio Cánovas del Castillo and José Canalejas y Méndez of Spain. We will discuss revolutionary violence later (Chapter Nine), but for thirty years or more, anarchist activity was a fact of political life. Most anarchists, of course, were never violent, and there was always a strong pacifist strain in anarchist thought.

Conrad was never a supporter of revolution or intellectually-driven change, even when it was non-violent. An early letter from 1885 deplores the victory of Gladstone's Liberals in the General Election that year, the first under an extension of the franchise and a redistribution of seats.

> By this time, you, I and the rest of the 'right thinking' have been grievously disappointed by the result of the General Election. The newly enfranchised idiots have satisfied the yearnings of Mr. Chamberlain's herd by cooking the national goose according to his recipe. The next culinary operation will be a pretty kettle of fish of an international character. Joy reigns in St. Petersburg, no doubt, and profound disgust in Berlin: the International Socialist Association are triumphant, and every disreputable ragamuffin in Europe feels that the day of universal brotherhood, despoliation and disorder is coming apace, and nurses day-dreams of well-plenished pockets amongst the ruin of all that is respectable, venerable and holy. The great British Empire went over the edge, and yet on to the inclined plane of social progress and radical reform. The downward movement is hardly perceptible yet, and the clever men who start it may flatter themselves with the progress; but they will soon find that the fate of the nation is out of their hands now! The Alpine avalanche rolls quicker and quicker as it nears the abyss — its ultimate destination! Where's the man to stop the crashing avalanche?

> Where's the man to stop the rush of social-democratic ideas? The opportunity and the day have come and are gone! Believe me: gone for ever! For the sun is set and the last barrier removed. England was the only barrier to the pressure of infernal doctrines born in continental back-slums. Now, there is nothing! The destiny of this nation and of all nations is to be accomplished in darkness amidst much weeping and gnashing of teeth, to pass through robbery, equality, anarchy and misery under the iron rule of a military despotism! Such is the lesson of common sense logic.

> Socialism must inevitably end in Caesarism.

Very rarely in literary or political history has so much bile been expended on a minority Liberal government. Quite a strong reaction, especially as Conrad was in Calcutta at the time and not even on the spot. He was in fact wholly wrong about the political situation; Gladstone's minority government fell six months later, and the Liberals lost 127 seats in the General Election of 1886, giving Lord Salisbury's Conservatives an overall majority. But Conrad's instincts are clear in his overwrought Jeremiad.

He remained opposed to the imposition of abstract ideas onto society, even as he cultivated more or less strong friendships with socialists of every stripe, for example making a pithy point while joshing H.G. Wells.

> The difference between us, Wells, is fundamental. You don't care for humanity but think they are to be improved. I love humanity but know they are not!

To his very good friend Cunninghame Graham, he wrote (in 1899):

> As to the peace meeting. If you want me to come I want still more to hear you. But, — I am not a peace man, not a democrat (I don't know what the word means really), and if I come, I shall go into the body of the hall. I want to hear you, — just as I want always to read you. ... When I was in Poland five years ago ... I preached at them and abused them for their social democratic tendencies. L'idée démocratique est un très beau phantome, and to run after it may be fine sport, but I confess I do not see what evils it is destined to remedy. It confers distinction on Messieurs Jaurès, Liebknecht & Co.[1] and your adhesion confers distinction upon it. International fraternity may be an object to strive for, and, in sober truth, since it has your support I will try to think it serious, but that illusion imposes by its size alone. Franchement, what would you think of an attempt to promote fraternity amongst people living in the same street, I don't even mention two neighbouring streets? Two ends of the same street.
>
> There is already as much fraternity as there can be — and that's very little and that very little is no good. What does fraternity mean? Abnegation — self-sacrifice — means something. Fraternity means nothing unless the Cain-Abel business. That's your true fraternity.

This is a direct attack on the sort of liberalism that abstracts away from community and postulates a broadly rational set of relation-

---

[1] Jean Jaurès (1859–1914) was a French socialist and pacifist, assassinated by a nationalist on the eve of the First World War. The Liebknechts were a family of socialist politicians; Conrad is probably referring to Wilhelm Liebknecht (1826–1900), one of the founders of the German SPD.

ships dictated by enlightened self-interest, a tradition created by thinkers such as John Stuart Mill, who wanted to develop our social and moral faculties to achieve a "higher level of existence", and in our own time, John Rawls.[2] The more radical implications of this have been teased out by several popular thinkers on the left, of whom Peter Singer, Professor of Bioethics at Princeton, is outstanding in his arguments that we have obligations to all humankind, not simply our family or community.[3] Singer argues that one has no greater ethical duties to members of one's family than to people one has never met, and that spending money on non-essential items is immoral as long as that money can be spent on alleviating poverty, disease or starvation elsewhere; one should be prepared to reduce oneself to something near the status of the poorest. This does follow from a certain commonly-held set of assumptions, and Singer is admirable in his devotion to consistency. "The notion that human life is sacred just because it's human life is medieval," he has said.[4] In a well-known interview, he even apologises for spending money on caring for his mother, ill with Alzheimer's disease. "I think this has made me see how the issues of someone with these kinds of problems are really very difficult. Perhaps it is more difficult than I thought before, because it is different when it's your mother."[5] This allowed right-wing commentator Peter Berkowitz to make the obvious rejoinder that "it is hard to imagine a more stunning rebuke to the well-heeled and well-ensconced academic discipline of practical ethics than that its most controversial and influential star, at the peak of his discipline, after an Oxford education, after twenty five years as a university professor, and after the publication of thousands of pages laying down clear cut rules on life-and-death issues, should reveal, only as the result of a reporter's prodding, and only in the battle with his own elderly mother's suffering, that he has just begun to appreciate that the moral life is complex."[6]

The intellectualisation of the drive for change is in itself problematic. As Marlow puts it:

---

[2]   John Rawls, *A Theory of Justice*, Oxford: Oxford University Press, 1971.
[3]   See for instance Peter Singer, 'Famine, affluence and morality', *Philosophy and Public Affairs*, 1(3), 1972, 229-243. For Singer's radical utilitarian philosophy as a whole, see Singer's website at http://www.princeton.edu/~psinger/.
[4]   Michael Specter, 'The dangerous philosopher', *New Yorker*, 6th Sept, 1999.
[5]   Specter, 'The dangerous philosopher'.
[6]   Peter Berkowitz, 'Other people's mothers: the utilitarian horrors of Peter Singer', *New Republic*, 10th Jan, 2000, 27-37.

> Hang ideas! They are tramps, vagabonds, knocking at the back-door of your mind, each taking a little of your substance, each carrying away some crumb of that belief in a few simple notions you must cling to if you want to live decently and would like to die easy.

Simplicity is a virtue in moral awareness. Ransome, in *The Shadow-Line*, lives by loyalty to his shipmates in one of Conrad's few attempts to sketch a positive outlook, while Prince Roman is sustained through his terrible troubles by "a fidelity without fear and without reproach". But moral ambition reaches beyond such basic possibilities, as the philosopher Stein tells Marlow, in his broken English.

> 'We want in so many different ways to be,' he began again. 'This magnificent butterfly finds a little heap of dirt and sits still on it; but man he will never on his heap of mud keep still. He want to be so, and again he want to be so. ...' He moved his hand up, then down. ... 'He wants to be a saint, and he wants to be a devil – and every time he shuts his eyes he sees himself as a very fine fellow – so fine as he can never be. ... In a dream. ...'[7]

Nevertheless, moral simplicity does not make the problem of behaving morally or judging action *easier*, and it is not intended to. Simple, straightforward moral codes do not mean that one can cut corners in moral diligence. In *The Secret Agent*, the "grand personage" Sir Ethelred demands abstract police reports. "Only no details, pray. Spare me the details". This abstraction means that he does not get all the facts needed for moral judgement, specifically how far the police are prepared to go in fostering contacts with the anarchists; it is in the details, as the expression tells us, where the devil is located. Similarly, Winnie Verloc does not ask difficult questions of her husband – until she belatedly discovers that he has been concealing the death of her brother Stevie. Making the right moral decisions demands time and seriousness.[8]

Supporting revolt

Lack of seriousness is one cause of the support for revolutions. Detestation of a particular government or situation may be perfectly proper – after all most toppled governments, from Tsar Nicholas's to the Shah of Iran's to Saddam Hussein's, generally deserve their

---

[7]   In *Lord Jim*. Conrad's ellipses.
[8]   George A. Panichas, *Joseph Conrad: His Moral Vision*, Macon, GA: Mercer University Press, 2005, 6.

fate. But the risk is concomitant destruction of the vital social connections, institutions and attitudes that any tenable social life requires. Blithely assuming that society will mould itself to top-down *diktat* is a precondition for dangerous creeds to spread. George Bush's White House, a place where moral seriousness is sometimes feigned but rarely in evidence, has already been the locus of exactly such slovenly thinking with respect to Iraq and Afghanistan. Afghanistan under the Taliban was such a ghastly place[9] that few would argue that regime change was not justified,[10] but expecting a flourishing civil society to emerge to order was cretinous.

Political vigilance, like moral vigilance, must be constant and thorough. In describing the career of Pedro Montero in *Nostromo*, Conrad sets out an all-too-plausible narrative about how a lazy, unintelligent man can engineer a revolution of which "the fundamental causes were the same as ever, rooted in the political immaturity of the people, in the indolence of the upper classes and the mental darkness of the lower." Worrying about the probity of politicians is important, but we cannot expect politicians to be effective, moral and public-spirited if citizens are not similarly serious about public affairs.[11]

One of Conrad's fascinating insights is how attractive revolutionary creeds are to people who, one would think, should be repelled by them. In the short story 'The informer', the narrator is told about the strange support that comfortable, well-off people give to revolutionary movements, support that still exists today as *Guardian* readers thrill to the latest derring-do of Subcomandante Marcos.

> 'Don't you know yet,' he said, 'that an idle and selfish class loves to see mischief being made, even if it is made at its own expense? Its own life being all a matter of pose and gesture, it is unable to realize the power and danger of a real movement and of words that have no sham meaning. It is all fun and sentiment. It is sufficient, for instance, to point out the attitude of the old French aristocracy towards the philosophers whose words were preparing the Great Revolution. Even in England, where you have some common-sense, a demagogue has only to shout loud enough and long enough to find some backing in the very class he is shouting at. ... The demagogue carries the amateurs of emotion with him. Amateurism in this, that, and the other thing is a delightfully

---

[9]   E.g. Peter Marsden, *The Taliban: War, Religion and the New Order in Afghanistan*, Karachi: Oxford University Press, 1998.

[10]   Cf. Kieron O'Hara, *After Blair: David Cameron and the Conservative Tradition*, Duxbury: Icon Books, 2007, 123-129.

[11]   O'Hara, *After Blair*, 269-276.

easy way of killing time, and of feeding one's own vanity — the silly vanity of being abreast with the ideas of the day after to-morrow.'

Another story produced at about the same time, 'An anarchist', finds a poor workman erroneously charged with revolutionary crimes after a boozy birthday celebration. His case might have been fairly straightforward, but ...

> ... whatever chance he had was done away with by a young socialist lawyer who volunteered to undertake his defence. In vain he assured him that he was no anarchist; that he was a quiet, respectable mechanic, only too anxious to work ten hours per day at his trade. He was represented at the trial as the victim of society and his drunken shoutings as the expression of infinite suffering. The young lawyer had his way to make, and this case was just what he wanted for a start. The speech for the defence was pronounced magnificent.
>
> The poor fellow paused, swallowed, and brought out the statement:
>
> 'I got the maximum penalty applicable to a first offence.'

Conrad is also sensitive to the way that revolutionary thinking is often conditioned by the very attitudes that are supposed to be overthrown. In *The Secret Agent*, the anarchist Michaelis has a Lady Patroness, who despises material interests, yet who hardly seems to have taken the revolutionary *point* on board. Her feelings are an odd mix of misplaced pity and compassion, and snobbery.

> She disliked the new elements of plutocracy in the social compound, and industrialism as a method of human development appeared to her singularly repulsive in its mechanical and unfeeling character. The humanitarian hopes of the mild Michaelis tended not towards utter destruction, but merely towards the complete economic ruin of the system. And she did not really see where was the moral harm of it. It would do away with all the multitude of the 'parvenus,' whom she disliked and mistrusted, not because they had arrived anywhere (she denied that), but because of their profound unintelligence of the world, which was the primary cause of the crudity of their perceptions and the aridity of their hearts. With the annihilation of all capital they would vanish too; but universal ruin (providing it was universal, as it was revealed to Michaelis) would leave the social values untouched. The disappearance of the last piece of money could not affect people of position.

Similarly, in *Under Western Eyes*, Mme de S —, who is bankrolling the organisation and running a salon for Peter Ivanovitch at the Château

Borel, is driven by a strong antipathy to the 'robbers' in the government who have taken her property, while the oppressed masses she merely finds vulgar. Meanwhile, Ivanovitch himself, the 'great feminist', is brutish in his treatment of women, especially Tekla. One remembers how much of the argument directed at Margaret Thatcher by the liberal elite was plainly sexist and snobbish, consisting of *ad hominem* attacks exploiting precepts to which they were nominally opposed. One recalls Jonathan Miller ("her odious suburban gentility and sentimental, saccharine patriotism, catering to the worst elements of commuter idiocy") and Mary Warnock appalled at her shopping at Marks & Spencer ("packaged together in a way that's not exactly vulgar, just low"). John Major and John Prescott have suffered similarly.

Indeed, much revolutionary thought trades on a somewhat snobbish detestation of suburban simplicity and stolidity, a snobbery with which *Under Western Eyes* is suffused. Conrad was the least suburban of men, and the charged atmosphere of Geneva as relayed by the narrator, in the company of the jaundiced Russian exiles, is hardly flattering. Nevertheless, the irony of the narration undercuts much of the negativity: their complaints about its being "indifferent and hospitable in its cold, almost scornful toleration – a respectable town of refuge to which all these sorrows and hopes were nothing" imply a political creed opposed to the human instincts of hospitality, respectability and refuge. The narrator later fulminates against:

> ... a solitary Swiss couple, whose fate was made secure from the cradle to the grave by the perfected mechanism of democratic institutions in a republic that could almost be held in the palm of one's hand. The man, colourlessly uncouth, was drinking beer out of a glittering glass; the woman, rustic and placid, leaning back in the rough chair, gazed idly around.

This is reminiscent of Harry Lime's puckish 'cuckoo clock' speech in *The Third Man*, and though Conrad enjoys his anti-Swiss rhetoric, the value of the Swiss couple's security is surely not negligible.

The effects of revolution

Aside from shattering security, what can revolution achieve? Conrad argues in many places that very little good will follow – societies are monolithic and resist change. Either the same or analogous hierarchies remain in place, in which case there is no obvious gain, or alternatively social structure is swept away with a dramatic loss of social cohesion. The teacher/narrator of *Under Western Eyes* has decided views on revolution, which he imparts to Natalia.

> The last thing I want to tell you is this: in a real revolution — not a simple dynastic change or a mere reform of institutions — in a real revolution the best characters do not come to the front. A violent revolution falls into the hands of narrow-minded fanatics and of tyrannical hypocrites at first. Afterwards comes the turn of all the pretentious intellectual failures of the time. Such are the chiefs and the leaders. You will notice that I have left out the mere rogues. The scrupulous and the just, the noble, humane, and devoted natures; the unselfish and the intelligent may begin a movement — but it passes away from them. They are not the leaders of a revolution. They are its victims: the victims of disgust, of disenchantment — often of remorse. Hopes grotesquely betrayed, ideals caricatured — that is the definition of revolutionary success. There have been in every revolution hearts broken by such successes.

The "Western eyes" of the narrator are not finely attuned to the problems facing the Russian revolutionaries. Politics is hard to judge for an outsider, and the option of shuffling the pack should no doubt be retained when the status quo is too awful to want to preserve.[12] But the 'Author's note' leaves us in no doubt of Conrad's opinion.

> [Utopians] are unable to see that all they can effect is merely a change of names. The oppressors and the oppressed are all Russians together; and the world is brought once more face to face with the saying that the tiger cannot change his stripes nor the leopard his spots.

Conrad pursued this theme throughout his career. Even as early as *An Outcast of the Islands,* the scheming of Babalatchi and Abdulla against the paternalist regime of Tom Lingard actually makes things worse for the Malay natives, thus foreshadowing themes from a number of stories, in particular *Nostromo.*

A more sinister example occurs in *Lord Jim,* where the *ad hoc* revolutionary coalition between Gentleman Brown and Kassim leads to disaster for them, in different ways, as well as for Jim. Jim and Gentleman Brown are outside forces, but Kassim's involvement makes things worse for his own people. The hijacking of revolutionary causes by "mere rogues" with a desire for violence is another factor in our ideological age. Lenin's regime was hardly a great idealistic success, but the bloody rule of Stalin that followed was an abomination that stands out even in the abominable 20th century. Nearer the

[12]   O'Hara, *After Blair.*

present, in Iraq, various insurgent groups, with more or less reason
to oppose the American invaders and the democratically-elected
government, have found their cause taken over by foreign nihilists
with loyalty to al Qaeda. That development has not been universally
welcomed. As one insurgent commander told an embedded, and
pretty fearless, *Guardian* reporter:

> 'We Sunni are to blame,' he said. 'In my area some ignorant
> al-Qaida guys have been kidnapping poor Shia farmers, killing
> them and throwing their bodies in the river. I told them: "This is
> not jihad. You can't kill all the Shia! This is wrong! The Shia mili-
> tias are like rabid dogs — why provoke them?"'

> Then he said: 'I am trying to talk to the Americans. I want to give
> them assurances that no one will attack them in our area if they
> stop the Shia militias from coming.'

> This man who had spent the last three years fighting the Ameri-
> cans was now willing to talk to them, not because he wanted to
> make peace but because he saw the Americans as the lesser of
> two evils. He was wrestling with the same dilemma as many
> Sunni insurgent leaders, beginning to doubt the wisdom of their
> alliance with al-Qaida extremists.[13]

In *Nostromo*, Conrad's most mature and profound reflection upon
this topic, Gould's attempt to shore up a liberal regime ultimately
fails; a scheme for the Occidental Province to secede from
Costaguana, dreamed up by the romantic intellectual Decoud, is
unravelling at the end of the novel — even Decoud's lover is advocat-
ing reunification. Should we even be surprised? Before the real
action of the novel begins, the deposition of brutish President
Guzman is followed by a recrudescence of politics, with a rise in
corruption and cynicism. Nation-building is hard, Conrad tells us,
because it is not a matter of adjusting the high politics at the top.
What Conrad really shares with Tolstoy is the sense that there is a
strong link between top and bottom, and readers of *Nostromo* would
not be surprised at any of the difficulties that we have seen not only
in Afghanistan or Iraq, but also in Bosnia or Timor-Leste, never mind
really tricky examples like the Democratic Republic of the Congo or
Somalia. Late 20th century politics was often a matter of reducing
the power of states, when they tyrannised populations and reduced
economic growth. There was a general trend of transferring powers

---

[13] Ghaith Abdul-Ahad, '"The Jihad is now against the Shias, not the
      Americans"', *The Guardian*, 13th Jan, 2007.

to non-state actors (often 'material interests').[14] But the removal of the *cause* of many of the problems (the Communist government in Yugoslavia, the kleptocracy of Joseph Mobutu, Saddam Hussein's brutal regime) has not solved those problems in many cases, and has often created new ones.

Altering top-level political activity won't necessarily have much of an effect at the lowest levels. No doubt there are strong connections between venality at the top and corruption down below, and getting rid of a bad regime might well remove one source of discord. But the connections between government and people are rarely negligible. Even somewhere like Rwanda, where a terrible massacre of Tutsi tribesmen by Hutus orchestrated by the government of Jean Kambanda took place in 1994, problematic social relations had to be in place for the opportunity for genocide to exist. Jared Diamond has argued that pressures over land added to the various political, racial and ideological influences to create an atmosphere where genocide could seem like an acceptable policy.[15]

Simply swapping governments won't, in many cases, have any effect on the politics of a country (which Tolstoy had also argued, at some length though with some implausibility, in *War and Peace*). Our propensity for action, our character, is not imposed from the top down. We will not become better people if our corrupt overlords are removed, even if our lives do as a matter of fact improve. This begs the question of what the roots of character actually *are*. Where should we look for the important influences?

---

[14] Francis Fukuyama, *State Building: Governance and World Order in the Twenty-First Century*, paperback edition, London: Profile Books, 2005.

[15] Jared Diamond, *Collapse: How Societies Choose to Fail or Survive*, London: Allen Lane, 2005.

Chapter Five

The Roots of Character I: Extremity

Conrad was very clear that action cannot simply be 'read off' character. It is an assumption often made that people have a 'character' which explains their actions. X is a good person, which is why he helped that old lady across the road. Y is a bad person, which is why she vandalised that telephone kiosk. Even our evaluation of an action will be affected by the character of the actor. Running a local neighbourhood watch scheme might be seen as benevolent protection or infernal busybodying, depending on who is doing it.

Conrad was clear that goodness and badness depend to a great extent on context, that the circumstances of an action are at least as important as the action itself, that one discovers one's character largely through action, and that one can change one's character if one works hard enough at it. Indeed, 'character' *per se* is aetiologically otiose—it doesn't *add* anything to our explanations of action.

The relationship between character and behaviour is one of the great mysteries of psychology, and it was a topic that Conrad explored exhaustively. In *Lord Jim*, Jim surprises himself by abandoning the *Patna* to its apparent fate. He could not have saved the lives of the 800 pilgrims on board, had it been sinking, but he found himself joining the Captain's escape—a dishonourable dereliction of duty, even if doing his duty could not possibly have benefited either him or any of the pilgrims. He didn't plan or intend to do it, but simply did. In *Under Western Eyes*, Razumov is astonished to be enlisted by Haldin in his plans for escape after he had assassinated a minister of state, and neither does he intend to betray him, until he does. In *Victory*, Heyst, who has renounced the world, finds himself acting 'out of character' by rescuing a damsel in distress, with fatal consequences for them both. Nostromo, "incorruptible", "indispensable", "tried and trusty", steals the Sulaco gold when he unexpectedly finds himself in sole charge. In the same novel, the dandyish Decoud behaves surprisingly heroically, and shows unsuspected commitment to the Sulacan cause. In the short story 'Falk', Falk finds his life blighted because, in extremity, he has "eaten man" – in fact he also kills the man he eats, but it is the *consumption* that ruins his future. In 'The secret sharer', Leggatt kills an insolent and workshy seaman during a tense moment in a hurricane. Conrad's *oeuvre* is laced with men faced with pressing dilemmas in extreme moments, where they discover some kind of truth about themselves. Nothing is the same again; their relationships with others are affected, but they also have the curse of a greater self-knowledge, undermining their ideal image. Sometimes the result has positive aspects, as when Leggatt swims away naked to a new life. Falk and Nostromo live unhappily with their transgressions. Heyst and Decoud court their own deaths. Jim and Razumov travel the world looking for redemption.

Jim is the most thoroughly explored; his character is a major aspect of the novel. He is physically the embodiment of the imperial hero.

> He was an inch, perhaps two, under six feet, powerfully built, and he advanced straight at you with a slight stoop of the shoulders, head forward, and a fixed from-under stare which made you think of a charging bull. His voice was deep, loud, and his manner displayed a kind of dogged self-assertion which had nothing aggressive in it. ... He was spotlessly neat, apparelled in immaculate white from shoes to hat, and in the various Eastern ports where he got his living as ship-chandler's water-clerk he was very popular.

As Marlow argues, appearances can deceive, with corrosive effects. One can even be fooled by one's own appearance, as Jim was.

> I would have trusted the deck to that youngster on the strength of a single glance, and gone to sleep with both eyes – and, by Jove! it wouldn't have been safe. There are depths of horror in that thought. He looked as genuine as a new sovereign, but there was some infernal alloy in his metal. How much? The least thing – the least drop of something rare and accursed; the least drop! – but he made you – standing there with his don't-care-hang air – he made you wonder whether perchance he were nothing more rare than brass.

The "depths of horror" are telling; in the ship-board community, reliability is all. Jim himself wants redemption, but also courts understanding. He protests to Marlow:

Have you watched a ship floating head down, checked in sinking
by a sheet of old iron too rotten to stand being shored up? Have
you? Oh yes, shored up? I thought of that—I thought of every
mortal thing; but can you shore up a bulkhead in five minutes—
or in fifty for that matter? Where was I going to get men that
would go down below? And the timber—the timber! Would you
have the courage to swing the maul for the first blow if you had
seen that bulkhead? Don't say you would: you have not seen it;
nobody would. Hang it—to do a thing like that you must believe
there is a chance, one in a thousand, at least, some ghost of a
chance; and you would not have believed. Nobody would have
believed. You think me a cur for standing there, but what would
you have done? What! You can't tell—nobody can tell. One must
have time to turn round. What would you have me do? Where
was the kindness in making crazy with fright all those people I
could not save single-handed—that nothing could save?

The situation was hopeless, and Jim argues that without hope action
is almost impossible. We should behave morally, but we are under
no obligation to be a saint or a hero.[1] Jim also argues that the extremity itself causes behaviour that cannot be anticipated.

What would you have done? You are sure of yourself—aren't
you? What would you do if you felt now—this minute—the
house here move, just move a little under your chair. Leap! By
heavens! you would take one spring from where you sit and land
in that clump of bushes yonder.

Character as regarded as a predictor of behaviour is an abstract concept; we decide, on the basis of (our own or others') character what
will happen in a set of circumstances, minimally described. The use
of character demands few assumptions, a stripped-down description of a world in which action can be seen as the output of a calculus.
But such descriptions are rarely of any use; Jim's rhetoric against
Marlow takes us out of the well-regulated, well-behaved abstract
and into the concrete world. What would Marlow do in *this* world
when *this* happens? "Trust a boat on the high seas to bring out the
Irrational that lurks at the bottom of every thought, sentiment, sen-
sation, emotion." Perhaps one of the aims of comfortable bourgeois
society is to make rational action possible, to provide the backdrop
of solidity against which behavioural calculi can operate consistently. But life generally is not like that, Conrad warns, and the sea is
an arena where ordinary people are often placed in extraordinary
conditions, and found out, for good or ill.

[1]   J.O. Urmson, 'Saints and heroes', in Joel Feinberg (ed.), *Moral Concepts*,
      Oxford: Oxford University Press, 1969, 60-73.

Jim's act of cowardice does not make him a criminal, and to judge isolated actions taken in extremity is unreasonably arbitrary. But *sui generis* incidents are often taken as indicators of someone's moral worth. It often happens that an action is praised or blamed as a result of circumstances quite out of the control of the actor, a phenomenon that Bernard Williams has called moral luck.[2] Again Marlow:

> Nothing more awful than to watch a man who has been found out, not in a crime but in a more than criminal weakness. The commonest sort of fortitude prevents us from becoming criminals in a legal sense; it is from weakness unknown, but perhaps suspected, as in some parts of the world you suspect a deadly snake in every bush — from weakness that may lie hidden, watched or unwatched, prayed against or manfully scorned, repressed or maybe ignored more than half a lifetime, not one of us is safe. We are snared into doing things for which we get called names, and things for which we get hanged, and yet the spirit may well survive — survive the condemnations, survive the halter, by Jove!

We are *named*, categorised as villain or hero. Marlow has sympathy for those whose moral luck is bad. In fact, he even goes so far as to blame the context: "there was a villainy of circumstances that cut these men [Jim and the white officers of the *Patna*] off more completely from the rest of mankind, whose ideal of conduct had never undergone the trial of a fiendish and appalling joke." Certainly Jim retains his self-image after his fateful jump — his travelling and his attempts to efface the memory shows that he still wishes, somehow, impossibly, to live up to his vision. Perhaps he comes close in the end, but his reluctance to take a more humble view of himself strongly suggests that his fatal flaw is less cowardice than Narcissism.

When the unlucky action is taken, the actor is suddenly de-socialised and bereft of support. Razumov, who was chronically undersocialised anyway, finds all his plans for advancement wrecked after he betrays Haldin. In 'The secret sharer', a young captain, new to his first ship, discovers a naked man in the sea next to his anchored ship. The man, Leggatt, has escaped his own ship after murdering a shipmate. The captain feels a sympathy for him, and hides him on board his ship; in fact, there is barely anywhere for him to hide, and he spends the voyage hidden awkwardly in the captain's small

---

[2]   Bernard Williams, 'Moral luck', in *Moral Luck*, Cambridge: Cambridge University Press, 1982, 20-39.

cabin, dodging the steward in his regular visits as best he can, until the captain, at great risk to his ship, engineers his escape.

Even before Leggatt appears, the captain is undergoing doubts of the sort that Jim never had.

> But what I felt most was my being a stranger to the ship; and if all the truth must be told, I was somewhat of a stranger to myself. The youngest man on board (barring the second mate), and untried as yet by a position of the fullest responsibility, I was willing to take the adequacy of the others for granted. They had simply to be equal to their tasks; but I wondered how far I should turn out faithful to that ideal conception of one's own personality every man sets up for himself secretly.

Leggatt has a story to tell not unlike Jim's (like Jim, he is a parson's son); he has departed from his own ideal conception in impossible circumstances, when his captain has panicked, and he needed help from a particularly truculent shipmate.

> It happened while we were setting a reefed foresail, at dusk. Reefed foresail! You understand the sort of weather. The only sail we had left to keep the ship running; so you may guess what it had been like for days. Anxious sort of job, that. He gave me some of his cursed insolence at the sheet. I tell you I was overdone with this terrific weather that seemed to have no end to it. Terrific, I tell you — and a deep ship. I believe the fellow himself was half crazed with funk. It was no time for gentlemanly reproof, so I turned round and felled him like an ox. He up and at me. We closed just as an awful sea made for the ship. All hands saw it coming and took to the rigging, but I had him by the throat, and went on shaking him like a rat, the men above us yelling, 'Look out! look out!'

Living in close proximity with Leggatt, the captain/narrator starts to identify with the other, and they form an intense bond. The captain even begins to see a "second self" in his companion. The two men grow close; Leggatt's bad luck could well, in different circumstances, be the captain's, which leads the captain to realise that his fidelity to his "ideal conception of [his] own personality" is inevitably contingent. Leggatt is completely alone, except for his double, and although the story ends positively, he leaves it as he entered it, naked, "to take his punishment: a free man, a proud swimmer striking out for a new destiny."

Heyst, the protagonist of *Victory*, has inherited a philosophy of rejecting human contact. He takes his father's dying advice, to "look on — make no sound", to avoid worldly ties, but he cannot sustain it through a lifetime. Simple humanity prevents him. In a farcical pre-

lude, he helps out Captain Morrison, who is so grateful that Heyst
cannot get rid of him. Heyst ends up on a sparsely populated island
with the rusting relics of his abandoned industrial venture, but ultimately cannot avoid another, more fateful, tie. On a visit to Surabaya
for supplies, he sees Lena, an untalented musical performer, being
mistreated by her impresario, and preyed upon sexually by the brutish innkeeper Schomberg; stricken with compassion and pity, he res-
cues her. He takes her to his island, where her love for him becomes
manifest; he can't find it within himself, however, to declare his love
for her, even though he is captivated by her voice and smile. A random set of circumstances — Heyst and Lena could only ever have
met fortuitously — has led to Heyst discovering his compassionate
nature. Lena wants his love, and she has it, did she but know it. But
he can only try to shore up his "ideal conception".

> It was naturally difficult for Heyst to keep his mind from dwell-
> ing on the nature and consequences of this, his latest departure
> from the part of an unconcerned spectator. Yet he had retained
> enough of his wrecked philosophy to prevent him from asking
> himself consciously how it would end. But at the same time he
> could not help being temperamentally, from long habit and from
> set purpose, a spectator still, perhaps a little less naïve but (as he
> discovered with some surprise) not much more farsighted than
> the common run of men. Like the rest of us who act, all he could
> say to himself, with a somewhat affected grimness, was:

> 'We shall see!'

Heyst's island idyll is destroyed by the arrival of three villains, sent
by the vengeful Schomberg. In the bloodletting that follows, Lena is
shot, and, dying in Heyst's arms, asks for a declaration of love; Heyst
cannot give it, still riven by doubt. He "bent low over her, cursing his
fastidious soul, which even at that moment kept the true cry of love
from his lips in its infernal mistrust of all life." In the end, he gives
only his impotent pity.

The meeting between Heyst and Lena, his rescue of her, was an
unpredictable event, but in the end his ideal conception had too
much power, whether "from long habit" or otherwise, for him to
surrender to his regard for Lena. The human ties did him no good —
but only because he tried to abjure ties. Heyst is not only opaque to
himself. He is habitually misunderstood throughout *Victory*, by the
unidentified narrator of Part One, by Schomberg who thinks he is a
Machiavellian villain, by Jones who thinks they are engaged in serious warfare, and not least by Lena who overestimates his commitment to her.

The notion of 'character' or 'personality' is a difficult one; how far can one pursue a life-project, create a notion of oneself, not in the abstract, but in the teeming, concrete, complex, dynamic world of people? Conrad's answer is only with a great deal of luck, moral and otherwise.

Chapter Six

The Roots of Character II: Labour

Work and character

When Conrad was writing, the 'lower orders', if they appeared in fiction at all, tended to be 'ruffians' or 'faithful retainers' in walk-on parts. Rarely did they have anything other than stereotypical lives or characters of their own. Some authors were more ambitious, but Conrad stands out. In many of his novels, especially the sea stories, working class men of coarse manners both good and bad receive careful and plausible characterisation. In the greatest example, *The Nigger of the "Narcissus"*, the crew of the *Narcissus* is rendered carefully, with several recognisably individual figures interacting together to weave the story of James Wait's strange death. We see gallows humour, spontaneous generosity, double-dealing, uncomplaining (and complaining) endurance, shirking, religiosity and lots of hard work.

For some reason due perhaps to the nature of the job, perhaps to the social class of its practitioners, the world of work has never featured strongly in Western literature. But Conrad, with his unique background, was a great believer in the importance, both to the individual and the community, of work and duty. In an essay about the merchant navy, Conrad argues that "A man is a worker. If he is not that, he is nothing."[1] Twenty years at sea, where the bad effects of shirking and laziness are immediately apparent, had made their mark, and he carried a strong work ethic over into his art (in the 'Author's note' to *The Nigger*, appropriately enough, he refers to himself as a "workman of art").

Much of his writing, particularly the non-fiction, tends towards the eulogistic, but is none the worse for that. In fiction he allows

---

[1] From '"Well done"'.

himself to be less didactic, and is more realistic, as with Marlow's "I don't like work — no man does — but I like what is in the work, — the chance to find yourself. Your own reality — for yourself, not for others — what no man can ever know."[2]

Life without work is seductive yet corrupting. Almayer is an example of someone with too much time to think and too little to do, while the spies in *The Secret Agent* are characterised by indolence and sponging off others. *The Shadow-Line*, a semi-autobiographical novel published in 1917, begins with the unnamed narrator believing he has lost interest in the sea, and abruptly resigning his position as first mate. Even though "I could not have been happier if I had had the life and the men made to my order by a benevolent Enchanter", he quits, "in that, to us, inconsequential manner in which a bird flies away from a comfortable branch." In retrospect, "My action, rash as it was, had more the character of divorce — almost of desertion." His decision goes down very badly with his fellow officers, and he is handed his papers at the harbour office "as if they had been my passports for Hades." On shore he finds himself incapable of staying at a 'landlubber's' hotel, preferring to remain in the Officers' Sailors' Home. Once again, Conrad warns us against intellectualising; the young man simply *thinks* too much. The many references to *Hamlet* in the text remind us of the young prince's fatal indecision. In the closing scene, the narrator's acquaintance Captain Giles puts the opposite, stoical view: "a man should stand up to his bad luck, to his mistakes, to his conscience, and all that sort of thing. ... Precious little rest in life for anybody. Better not think of it."

The irresponsible act almost scuppers the young man's opportunity to begin his first command, as important messages fail to get to him. As it is, he is late for the craft to take him to his ship. As he exercises his responsibilities, he begins to see that his new life as a captain is making new demands, and he is being moulded in new and unpredictable ways. "One goes on. And the time, too, goes on — till one perceives ahead a shadow-line warning one that the region of early youth, too, must be left behind." This had always been an important message for Conrad, and is the theme of the early story 'Youth', but here there is an explicit link between the end of youth, and the beginning of work, responsibility and challenge. The piece was all the more poignant as *The Shadow-Line* was Conrad's most substantial work of the Great War, when so many young men crossed their own shadow-line, and so few returned in "the supreme

---

[2]   From 'Youth'.

trial of a whole generation."[3] The novel is dedicated to Borys Conrad, then fighting in France.

The new captain's decisions and responsibilities, like the events that entangle Jim and Razumov, are life-changing, but differ in that they are not singularities but *connected series* of events, and therefore the results appear to be *changes* (or reconstructions) of character, rather than departures from it or revelations of previously unsuspected aspects of it. He is tested, and when the crew is struck down by fever, feels an unwarranted guilt. But the ship's cook, Ransome, one of the few men spared, is an indispensable aid throughout the voyage, despite his weak heart.

The sea as an end in itself

The basis of Ransome's fidelity, respect for his craft, and solidarity with his ailing shipmates, cannot be obligation. One is not obliged to be a saint. But it is part of the liberating nature of work, and the strength of the connections between the men on board. In *The Nigger of the "Narcissus"*, as Brian Richardson has pointed out in a perceptive essay,[4] Conrad uses a number of narratorial innovations to convey a sort of collective consciousness, usually but not exclusively expressed by a single crew member. The early stages of the novel use a third-person narrator with occasional interjections that imply that the narrator is actually one of the crew, though not one who has featured in the action ("Mr Baker ... kept all our noses to the grindstone"). Furthermore, the narrator uses Christian names of the 'good' crew members, surnames of the older sailors or the bad ones, and respectful titles ('Mr', 'Captain') for the officers, rather as a crewman with a sense of hierarchy and authority would. When the voyage begins, the usual pronoun used to refer to the crew shifts from 'they' to 'we', and occasionally back again when referring to them as a group of individuals, rather than a coherent unit. 'We' are engaged on particular collaborative tasks, such as the attempt to free Wait when he is trapped in the flooded forecastle. 'They' argue amongst themselves, or with 'their' officers. At the end of the novel, when the *Narcissus* has docked and the crew is dispersing, suddenly the narra-

---

[3]   From the 'Author's note' to *The Shadow-Line*.
[4]   Brian Richardson, 'Conrad and posthumanist narration: fabricating class and consciousness onboard the *Narcissus*', in Carola M. Kaplan, Peter Lancelot Mallios & Andrea White (eds.), *Conrad in the Twenty-First Century: Contemporary Approaches and Perspectives*, New York: Routledge, 2005, 213-222.

tor becomes 'I' — with the payoff line "I never saw them again" indicating that the skein of relationships, though very close during the voyage, remains highly contingent. Nevertheless, this narrator, seemingly identified firmly as an unnamed and undescribed crew member, also gives us impeccable third person descriptions of events that he could not have witnessed, such as meetings between Donkin and Wait, and juxtaposes the first and third person in such a way as to undermine any sense of realism.

This set of effects underlines the sense of temporary and contingent solidarity on the voyage. In particular, Conrad plays with the narration when Donkin tries to arouse the crew after Wait is denied permission to rejoin them. He uses the passive ("A lot of disputes seemed to be going on all around." "The hurtling flight of some heavy object was heard"), and tempers the use of the third person plural with ironic use of the first (the *Narcissus* "carried Singleton's completed wisdom, Donkin's delicate susceptibilities, and the conceited folly of us all."). The period of false consciousness of the crew, as an undervalued and underprivileged independent union, is marked by this combination of third person, passive construction, and ironic first person. Donkin spreads a democratic myth which is entertained by many of the crew ("the younger school of advanced thought"), and which is found persuasive in the heat of the moment. But eventually, Donkin's propaganda is resisted, as the revolutionary talk turns to violence, and the anti-establishment forces turn on each other. This miniature revolution blows itself out, like a storm. The crew's normally sound judgement deserts them at their revolutionary moment, whereupon they have no coherent plan of action or even a sensible and achievable goal.

Conrad's sense of the rightness of the solidarity of the crew in its relationship with the *Narcissus* itself involves a hierarchical view, not through love of hierarchies themselves, but rather through a sense of the fitness of things. Wait's disruption of the careful balance of the social relationships on the *Narcissus* is dangerous — akin to that of the Machiavellian characters in Shakespeare such as Edmund, Iago and Falconbridge — as the uncertainly with regard to his health and motives spreads an insidious corruption through the crew.

Donkin, the rebel, is a more directly negative character. But Brian Richardson, whose analysis of *The Nigger*'s narrative strategies is exemplary, betrays a certain lack of comprehension of Conrad's world view in his worries about Donkin's treatment at his creator's hands.

> [Conrad] also makes Donkin *both* a contemptible, lazy, selfish shirker *and* a spokesperson for socialist ideals — two types that while independently plausible, are historically unlikely as conjoined within the same person (labor organizing was, and is, a most altruistic activity), and here especially resonate as the stigmatic hybrid imagining of a conservative or reactionary.[5]

Seated at his desk at the University of Maryland, the good Professor has presumably never encountered labour organisers at their worst, but he might have watched *On the Waterfront*. And his blithe assumption that he knows more about labour relations than a man who had served as a merchant seaman for twenty years is stunning.

In today's context, opposition to trade unionism usually goes with a pro-capitalist or neo-liberal ideology, but as we have seen, Conrad's view of 'material interests' was a dim one, and he preferred value systems other than money. The ingestion of the merchant fleet by the capitalist system was a highly retrograde step, in his opinion. When the *Shadow-Line*'s young captain receives his commission, he is rather surprised to discover that he has been ensnared by the *ennui* of routine.

> I perceived that my imagination had been running in conventional channels and that my hopes had always been drab stuff. I had envisaged a command as a result of a slow course of promotion in the employ of some highly respectable firm. The reward of faithful service. Well, faithful service was all right. One would naturally give that for one's own sake, for the sake of the ship, for the love of the life of one's own choice; not for the sake of the reward.

> There is something distasteful in the notion of a reward.

The capitalist-inspired decline in the quality of the seagoing life is symbolised, for Conrad, by the switch from sail to steam. What he called "the spirit of modern hurry" (in *The Shadow-Line*) alienates the seaman from his labour, as he argues in the greatest of his non-fiction works, *The Mirror of the Sea*.

> The hurry of the times, the loading and discharging organization of the docks, the use of hoisting machinery which works quickly and will not wait, the cry for prompt dispatch, the very size of his ship, stand nowadays between the modern seaman and the thorough knowledge of his craft.

Sail has an aesthetic that steam cannot match.

---

[5]   Richardson, 'Conrad and posthumanist narration', 215.

The efficiency of a steamship consists not so much in her courage as in the power she carries within herself. It beats and throbs like a pulsating heart within her iron ribs, and when it stops, the steamer, whose life is not so much a contest as the disdainful ignoring of the sea, sickens and dies upon the waves. The sailing-ship, with her unthrobbing body, seemed to lead mysteriously a sort of unearthly existence, bordering upon the magic of the invisible forces, sustained by the inspiration of life-giving and death-dealing winds.

Sail respects the sea, and keeps men in a proper relation to it, as for example in this passage from *An Outcast of the Islands*. I use the word 'men' advisedly.

The sea of the past was an incomparably beautiful mistress, with inscrutable face, with cruel and promising eyes. The sea of today is a used-up drudge, wrinkled and defaced by the churned-up wakes of brutal propellers, robbed of the enslaving charm of its vastness, stripped of its beauty, of its mystery and of its promise.

The coming of steam, routine and regulations into the seafaring life produces a radical discontinuity between early and modern sailors.

But the seaman of the last generation, brought into sympathy with the caravels of ancient time by his sailing-ship, their lineal descendant, cannot look upon those lumbering forms navigating the naïve seas of ancient woodcuts without a feeling of surprise, of affectionate derision, envy, and admiration. For those things, whose unmanageableness, even when represented on paper, makes one gasp with a sort of amused horror, were manned by men who are his direct professional ancestors.

No; the seamen of three hundred years hence will probably be neither touched nor moved to derision, affection, or admiration. They will glance at the photogravures of our nearly defunct sail-ing-ships with a cold, inquisitive and indifferent eye. Our ships of yesterday will stand to their ships as no lineal ancestors, but as mere predecessors whose course will have been run and the race extinct. Whatever craft he handles with skill, the seaman of the future shall not be our descendant, but only our successor.[6]

The point of seamanship is not joy or adventure for its own sake. Reward, so "distasteful", is not to be replaced with the mere love of adventure. The point, rather, is faithful service, of the sort that Ransome provides.

---

[6]   From *The Mirror of the Sea*.

I venture to affirm that the main characteristic of the British men spread all over the world, is not the spirit of adventure so much as the spirit of service. I think that this could be demonstrated from the history of great voyages and the general activity of the race. That the British man has always liked his service to be adventurous rather than otherwise cannot be denied, for each British man began by being young in his time when all risk has a glamour. Afterwards, with the course of years, risk became a part of his daily work; he would have missed it from his side as one misses a loved companion.

The mere love of adventure is no saving grace. It is no grace at all. It lays a man under no obligation of faithfulness to an idea and even to his own self. Roughly speaking, an adventurer may be expected to have courage, or at any rate may be said to need it. But courage in itself is not an ideal. A successful highwayman showed courage of a sort, and pirate crews have been known to fight with courage or perhaps only with reckless desperation in the manner of cornered rats. There is nothing in the world to prevent a mere lover or pursuer of adventure from running at any moment. There is his own self, his mere taste for excitement, the prospect of some sort of gain, but there is no sort of loyalty to bind him in honour to consistent conduct.[7]

Conrad's work ethic, where money or thrills are less of a reward than the joy of a good job well done, is an aristocratic one, and one with heavy moral overtones.

Overcoming obstacles

The symbolism of a small community alone in a ship on the boundless ocean is obvious, and Conrad made much of it. "For what is the array of the strongest ropes, the tallest spars, and the stoutest canvas against the mighty breath of the infinite, but thistle stalks, cobwebs and gossamer?"[8] The smallness of man and the immensity of the world was a constant theme in Conrad; the Malay and Congolese jungles served the same symbolic purpose.

In such an environment, work develops in tandem with conditions; the job one does is designed to achieve what one needs to achieve. Practice within a context results in skill and success, and a level of attainment that should be a beacon for others. Again in *The Mirror*, Conrad discusses the yachting industry (not something he,

---

[7]   From '"Well done"', Conrad speaking with his own voice in a piece of non-fiction.

[8]   From *The Mirror of the Sea*.

"a man who had but little to do with pleasure sailing", poses as an expert on).

Now, the moral side of an industry, productive or unproductive, the redeeming and ideal aspect of this bread-winning, is the attainment and preservation of the highest possible skill on the part of the craftsmen. Such skill, the skill of technique, is more than honest; it is something wider, embracing honesty and grace and rule in an elevated and clear sentiment, not altogether utilitarian, which may be called the honour of labour. It is made up of accumulated tradition, kept alive by individual pride, rendered exact by professional opinion, and, like the higher arts, it is spurred on and sustained by discriminating praise.[9]

This is why the attainment of proficiency, the pushing of your skill with attention to the most delicate shades of excellence, is a matter of vital concern. Efficiency of a practically flawless kind may be reached naturally in the struggle for bread. But there is something beyond — a higher point, a subtle and unmistakeable touch of love and pride beyond mere skill; almost an inspiration which gives to all work that finish which is almost art — which *is* art.

Language, like practice, is similarly honed: Conrad writes (in *The Mirror*) of "a sailor's phrase which has all the force, precision, and imagery of technical language that, created by simple men with keen eyes for the real aspect of the things they see in their trade, achieves the just expression seizing upon the essential, which is the ambition of the artist in words." Practice, language, ritual, initiative and authority: all these enable the seafarer to get the ship from A to B. In such circumstances, the democratic ideal is not actually as remote as the strong reaction to Donkin's rabble-rousing in *The Nigger* would seem to suggest. But equality in the context of the structure of authority-relations, with proper regard for the expertise of different mariners properly fostered, nourished and combined, is the ideal. Power is not the issue; rather, it is merit, of the system, of the technology, and of the seamen: "discipline is not ceremonious in merchant ships, where the sense of hierarchy is weak, and where all feel them-

---

[9]   This description is strikingly reminiscent of the sociological idea of the community of practice, currently studied a great deal in management science and knowledge engineering. Etienne Wenger, *Communities of Practice: Learning, Meaning and Identity*, Cambridge: Cambridge University Press, 1998. For a description of the task of navigation from the disciplines of anthropology and cognitive psychology, see Edwin Hutchins, *Cognition in the Wild*, Cambridge, MA: MIT Press, 1995.

selves equal before the unconcerned immensity of the sea and the exacting appeal of the work."[10]

These issues are explored in some depth in 'Typhoon', where once again Conrad uses a little bit of self-conscious literary trickery, this time playing with genre. The basic story, of the attempt by Capt. MacWhirr and his British crew to sail through a colossal storm, and incidentally to save the lives of 200 Chinese coolies returning to their homeland after working on a construction project, is a classic, if minor, adventure yarn where the sophisticated, stoical, white authority figures protect the interests of non-white others who are too unenlightened to act in their own interests. It even featured in an omnibus book called *Four Sensational Adventure Novels*[11] probably assembled in the 1930s together with three other melodramatic and exotically-located works by Francis Brett Young, H. de Vere Stacpoole and Dale Collins. But there is much more to it than that. MacWhirr is extraordinarily ordinary; he has "just enough imagination to carry him through each successive day, and no more." Seen through the eyes of his younger, less conventional shipmates, he begins the story as a comic figure. He cannot believe, despite warnings, that the approaching storm is one of the worst seen in the region; he refuses to countenance the possibility that its severity will be something literally out of his previous experience. As a result, he disregards his seamanship manual's advice to sail around the tumult, but instead faces the weather head on. The storm is every bit as severe as the warning signs suggested, and Conrad's description of the sailors' efforts to sail through it is dramatic, exciting and, as ever, convincing.

Meanwhile, as the coolies' luggage has come adrift, they fight over their money and possessions, and as the storm gets worse, MacWhirr sends a party of seamen down to restore order. But as the typhoon reaches its height, Conrad simply drops the narrative – the reader misses the worst of the storm, and instead there is a jump cut to the ship having sailed through and reached its destination. This is unthinkable in an adventure story along straightforward genre lines, and alerts us to the fact that although there is a great deal of adventure in the story – after all, extreme conditions at sea are undeniably adventurous – that is not what Conrad is interested in.

What, then, is he writing about? Shorn of the climax of the storm, what we are left with is MacWhirr's stolid failure to realise the dan-

[10] From *The Nigger of the "Narcissus"*.
[11] *Four Sensational Adventure Novels*, London: Odhams, n.d.

ger the ship was in, and the end result, which was that his seamanship took it through. Furthermore, he had the presence of mind and calmness to sort out the fighting; at the end of the tale, MacWhirr distributes the scattered money to the coolies in equal shares, not the best or most imaginative of solutions, but a practical and equitable one. The conclusion, that "he got out of it very well for such a stupid man" is a sideways tribute to the value of stupidity (or, better, the cost of cleverness) and the way that imagination is sometimes a little over-rated. Furthermore, MacWhirr does not work in a vacuum; there is a crew, there is his (and their) experience, and there is a method. Conrad reiterates one of the lessons of *The Nigger of the "Narcissus"* that heroism and democracy are all very well, but that the world gets by on unglamorous work well done.

Chapter Seven

The Roots of Character III: Community

The working community is an important locus of and influence on character. But work, though a good symbol for life in a society, is not a perfect one. The fact that there are many more women in the workforce now than when Conrad was writing makes his discussions of society in terms of work and the work ethic somewhat more inclusive than he had intended. He certainly appreciated that women worked hard to achieve things 'behind the scenes', as, for instance, Marlow's aunt who gets him his job in 'Heart of darkness', but he also viewed (middle class) women as crucially cut off from key aspects of society by their banishment from the workplace. This was hardly true when he was writing his great books, and anyway the First World War changed attitudes to women working forever. It may be that Conrad, miraculously transported into the 21st century, would appreciate (or be driven to appreciate) this social change, and modify his misogyny.

Another important disanalogy between a ship (or a workplace) and life in general is that work has a purpose, or a function, while life does not.[1] In the workplace we have some kind of contractual or quasi-contractual relationship with our bosses. There are, of course, many political philosophers, such as Hobbes, Locke and Rousseau, who have held a similar view about our relationship with wider society and such thinkers would naturally be happier with Conrad's use of the workplace metaphor. However, for a conservative thinker like Conrad, suspicious of the idea of an 'end' to history, or human endeavour, and highly critical of the abstract thought that assumes a purpose or function for society, the metaphor cannot be perfect. His

[1]   Cf. Kieron O'Hara, *After Blair: David Cameron and the Conservative Tradition*, Duxbury: Icon Books, 2007.

aristocratic interpretation of the ideals of fidelity and service go some distance to bridging the gap — he argues that contracts should not govern all aspects of working relationships either, particularly with respect to doing "faithful service". But we should also expect to find Conrad pondering more directly on the communities into which we are born or brought, those which we do not choose, and those which do not have a precise function, where the contractual relationship is inappropriate.

Nation

It is unsurprising that Conrad thought a lot about nationality. His experience as a Polish national, "that nationality not so much alive as surviving, which persists in thinking, breathing, speaking, hoping, and suffering in its grave railed in by a million of bayonets and triple-sealed with the seals of three great empires"[2], was deeply traumatic. Yet of course Conrad was also, his strong accent apart, almost an 'English gentleman.' He was an accomplished stylist of the English language; he lived most of his life in the rural South-East of England; he was offered, and declined, honours, and gave up his civil list pension to help the British war effort; before that he had been a member of the British mercantile marine. After he left Poland in 1874, he returned only occasionally, even after he had been released from his status as Russian citizen. The essay 'Poland revisited' tells the story of the trip made with his family in 1914, and is an impressive meditation on the role of memory in a world in turmoil (the Conrads were trapped in Central Europe by the outbreak of war) with Conradian expressions of guilt explicitly about the legitimacy of the role of the writer in such times, and also, implicitly, about his apparent renunciation of Polish history and language.

Conrad had apparently been wounded by a verbal attack from a well-known novelist, Eliza Orzeszkowa, in 1899, who had argued strongly (in the context of a heated Polish political debate of the time) that those with artistic ability (as opposed to mere manual workers) should not leave Poland, but should stay to help with the preservation and continuity of Polish national culture. She had singled Conrad out for opprobrium, and suggested that he wrote in English because of the greater amount of money available for an English-language writer (ironically given Conrad's wretched financial state). Much of his self-mythologising (for instance, about his

[2]   From 'Prince Roman'.

decision to become a writer in English, which he always played down), may well have stemmed from this early slight.

Perhaps his most poignant fictionalisation of the Polish plight is the story of 'Prince Roman', where the eponymous prince – who disdainfully remarks of the Russian imperial family "Those people had never been heard of when our house was already illustrious" – represents the ideals of honour and service that Conrad always admired and extolled. Prince Roman, having given up his liberty and position by fighting the Russians, is exiled in defeat, and only allowed to return to Poland when an old man, deaf and weak. His children are uninterested in him. But still he exudes authority, and continues his service to the nation. The framing narrative consists of a older narrator telling the tale of how he, as a young boy, met the elderly Prince, exactly as the young Conrad met the Polish patriot Prince Roman Sanguszko at his Uncle Tadeusz's residence in 1866. The story is idealistic, but moving, realistic about the ambivalence that many Poles must have felt about the apparently hopeless cause of independence, and clearly heartfelt.

Exile was explored in 'Amy Foster', a short story from the *Typhoon* volume, which tells the tale of a would-be Polish emigrant to America, shipwrecked on the Kent coast. As the sole survivor, his appearance in a little Kentish village, gibbering desperately, terrifies the locals. Amy Foster is a local girl, the only person to be kindly towards him; they eventually marry. No-one can find out his name properly – Yanko Goorall is their best guess. Yanko and Amy begin a happy life, with a son, but linguistic and cultural barriers separate them; Amy objects when Yanko tries to teach their son Polish. They begin to drift apart, and events reach a climax when Yanko falls ill, and becomes delirious and feverish; when he reverts to his native tongue to cry for water, Amy interprets this as mad, threatening rage and runs away. Without care, Yanko dies.

We should be wary as to how far we see Yanko's experiences as a caricature of Conrad's own as a Pole in exile in Kent; after all, the former was an ignorant peasant. But equally, Yanko was the only explicitly Polish character featured in Conrad's fiction outside 'Prince Roman' ('Amy Foster' was written in 1901, 'Prince Roman' in 1910), and there is evidence that early drafts made stronger connections between Conrad himself and his literary invention.[3] National-

[3]   Gail Fraser, 'Conrad's revisions to "Amy Foster"', *Conradiana*, 20 (1988), 181-193.

ity was a strong influence on Conrad, and an important factor in the roots of character.

Polishness was a difficult subject for Conrad, and he was happier addressing it in his non-fiction. He found writing about Englishness somewhat easier, perhaps being an Anglophile outsider. The scepticism of Marlow, the pettifogging and small-mindedness of the teacher of English in *Under Western Eyes*, the hopeless romanticism of Jim, the devotion to duty of the crew of the *Narcissus*, are all renderings of various good and bad aspects of the English. Conrad's Englishmen were rarely high-born — most of the characters we meet in Conrad are businessmen and seamen. Big political figures, such as Sir Ethelred, the great personage of *The Secret Agent*, feature rarely and are rarely agreeable.

Ironically, his deepest exploration of nationality, character, action, morality and belief was his analysis of Russia in *Under Western Eyes*, his merciless unpicking of the suspicion, treachery and arbitrariness of the country that presumed to rule Poland. In his description of "senseless desperation provoked by senseless tyranny" Conrad depicts something that almost looks like a failed state of our own day, a place that is not only run badly, but which also acts as a breeding ground and exporter of the revolutionary virus. Yet Russia is an ideal which Conrad can appreciate. Razumov is illegitimate, and so lacks any kind of familial support. He is also quiet, taciturn and withdrawn. He explains all this in an outburst to Haldin.

'You are a son, a brother, a nephew, a cousin — I don't know what — to no end of people. I am just a man. Here I stand before you. A man with a mind. Did it ever occur to you how a man who had never heard a word of warm affection or praise in his life would think on matters on which you would think first with or against your class, your domestic tradition — your fireside prejudices? ... Did you ever consider how a man like that would feel? I have nothing to think against. My tradition is historical. What have I to look back to but that national past from which you gentlemen want to wrench away your future? Am I to let my intelligence, my aspirations towards a better lot, be robbed of the only thing it has to go upon at the will of violent enthusiasts? You come from your province, but all this land is mine — or I have nothing. No doubt you shall be looked upon as a martyr some say — a sort of hero — a political saint. But I beg to be excused. I am content in fitting myself to be a worker. And what can you people do by scattering a few drops of blood on the snow? On this Immensity. On this unhappy Immensity! I tell you,' he cried, in a vibrating, subdued voice, and advancing one step nearer the bed, 'that what it needs is not a lot of haunting phantoms that I could walk through — but a man!'[4]

Misunderstanding between nations and cultures seems to be almost inevitable — a theme dating back to Conrad's earliest novels. In *Almayer's Folly*, Almayer is unable to see the growing importance of Nina's Malay identity to her, and equally unable to overlay it with European education; while in *An Outcast of the Islands*, Willems declares his love for the pirate's daughter Aïssa by imploring "Let us go away from here. Go very far away! Very far; you and I!" to which she reacts with shame and horror, as if he wishes to hide her away. Perhaps Conrad's view of cultural misunderstanding is one reply to Chinua Achebe's charge that he fails to advance the Africans' interests; how could he possibly know what those interests are?

The activities of the Eastern spies *Under Western Eyes* are explicitly presented by the title as problematic. The fellowship of liberal and social-democratic thinkers is shown to be a myth. Haldin's abstract thought sits on top of a solid social and familial background, which he has the choice of embracing or reacting against. Razumov argues that Haldin has, in common with humanity as a whole, several reference points that he can "think against." The 'phantoms' he refers to are the ungrounded, unlocated, unreal abstract 'men' of political theory. We can think hard about morals, actions, ideals, but without a concrete meaningful context such thinking is merely hot air.

> 'And unfathomable mysteries! Can you conceive secret places in Eternity? Impossible. Whereas life is full of them. There are secrets of birth, for instance. One carries them on to the grave. There is something comical ... but never mind. And there are secret motives of conduct. A man's most open actions have a secret side to them. That is interesting and so unfathomable! For instance, a man goes out of a room for a walk. Nothing more trivial in appearance. And yet it may be momentous. He comes back — he has seen perhaps a drunken brute, taken particular notice of the snow on the ground — and behold he is no longer the same man. The most unlikely things have a secret power over one's thoughts — the grey whiskers of a particular person — the goggle eyes of another.'[5]

All these, the drunken brute, the grey whiskers, the goggle eyes, have been encountered by Razumov in his 'walk', which began as an attempt to save Haldin, and ended as a betrayal. As the remainder of

[4]   Conrad's ellipsis.
[5]   Conrad's ellipsis.

Under Western Eyes so graphically demonstrates, Haldin's assertion that "Men like me leave no posterity" is absolutely false.

Community

Razumov is unusual in that his *only* community is his nation, but Conrad had the usual exile's difficulties in finding a local home to accompany and complement his national feeling. He found himself in the circumscribed seaborne communities in the mercantile marine, and his work ethic is therefore tangled up in much of his thinking about community, but it goes without saying that a ship's crew is an unusual type of community. It is limited in size; it has little or no contact for weeks on end with other communities; it contains no women; it has a goal (the port it is to reach, the safe conduct of its cargo). It is an unusual type of work: failure to do one's job well could result in death for all the crew; the crew live together and have no home life except that between voyages.

Conrad's most sustained exploration of shorebound community was in his final completed novel, *The Rover*, set in the port of Toulon during the revolutionary war with Britain. The dramatic events of the revolution are alluded to, but play no immediate part in the action; the story begins in 1796 when fervour is declining, three years after the slaughter precipitated by the Siege of Toulon (where the young Napoleon first attained fame), during which hundreds and possibly thousands of royalists were killed by victorious revolutionaries. To this wounded city, Jean Peyrol returns to retire, after a 40 year career of piracy; he arrives at sunrise, draped in the French flag. He finds a remote farmhouse where he is allowed to stay by the emotionally damaged Arlette, who took part in the massacre, even though her parents were killed in it. She is being courted by Scevola, a barbaric and fanatical revolutionary, who enjoyed the violence of the revolution itself but is becoming disenchanted with the stability that is slowly returning.

Eight years later, Peyrol has become part of a community, with commitments — like Odysseus, his wandering days are over. Toulon needs social solidarity; it is blockaded by the English navy. He and the other occupants of the farm are joined by Lt. Réal, a Razumov-like figure, a French officer lacking ties of his own. Réal and Arlette fall in love, though each for their different reasons finds this hard; in particular, Réal is handed a secret mission authorised by Napoleon himself to deceive the English with fake documents. Scevola jealously plots Réal's murder. After an action-packed and extremely complicated night with several parallel narrative strands, Peyrol manages to wind up the loose ends successfully, carrying out Réal's mission at the cost of his own life (at sunset), so that Réal and Arlette can marry. The novel's coda shows France at peace, and the couple happily married and reminiscing about Peyrol and his "great heart".

Peyrol is, to an extent, a complimentary figure to Heyst from *Victory*. He discovers that commitment and action go together, that ties do bind. He finds himself in a number of relationships – the enemy of Scevola, the mentor of Réal, protector of Arlette (albeit with some erotic feeling for her too), and as the friend to a number of other characters. These relationships give him a reason for living, which his piratical existence did not – but a reason for living is also, paradoxically, a reason for dying, and he finds himself helping the French cause, ridding the world of Scevola and clearing away the obstacles to Réal's and Arlette's happiness. Compare that to Heyst's life of observation, commentary and not taking part: he dies misunderstood, for no purpose.

Peyrol, the rover, finds a meaning for his life and death in Toulon, in fidelity to a community, and patriotism for the nation. He has no ideals beyond that, and yet is able to act heroically, and to be remembered. He does not intellectualise his situation – he observes a simple loyalty to those around him, and to France. The abstract ideals of the revolution – liberty, equality, fraternity – mean nothing to him, and are shown to be meaningless without a concrete setting. The brutish Scevola, the local Jacobin, is an eye-rolling caricature whom Conrad hardly treats seriously, but even Lt. Réal becomes capable of warmth and action *only* when he has immersed himself in life in Toulon. He has been orphaned by the revolution, and is planning to use his secret mission as an excuse to avoid commitment to Arlette, before Peyrol outthinks him and goes on the mission himself.

Conrad's epigraph for *The Rover* is taken from Spenser's *The Faerie Queene*, and expresses the simple pleasure, relief and peace that Peyrol finds.

Sleep after toyle, port after stormie seas,
Ease after warre, death after life, does greatly please.

These lines are inscribed on Conrad's tomb in Canterbury.

Final thoughts on character

Conrad was certainly not a determinist in any sense, and never set down anything that one could call a psychological theory. Some of his most important characters were relatively functional and unidimensional — notably various evil figures in his work, such as Scevola, Mr Jones and Ricardo from *Victory*, and Gentleman Brown from *Lord Jim*. Conrad's women are notably and obviously less realised than his men, and Conrad's narrators even sometimes tacitly assume that the reader is a man — the late novel *The Arrow of Gold* is at one point addressed to "those who know women".

But Conrad did think hard about idealism, self-image and action. Theories about action, particularly political theories, were of little value, for him, because they would always founder on the reefs of reality. The abstract man might do X because it is rational, and with a little shaking up of the incentives available to him in his particular epistemological state he might be induced to do Y. So much might be plausible on paper. Ideals can drive action, thanks to disengaged emotions such as guilt or pity.

Nevertheless, real people are embedded in reality — including national and communitarian ties of love and fidelity, work, skill and the relationships that they subtend, and sudden, unpredictable, one-off events of unusual magnitude. This makes human nature not hard but impossible to generalise about. So what, then, is a political thinker or actor to do?

Chapter Eight

Pessimism, Scepticism and Meaning

Conrad's art is multi-faceted, and it would be wrong to characterise him as a philosophical or political novelist bent on producing, testing and affirming hypotheses in his work, but among other things he was engaged in two important ideological tasks. He wished to affirm many of the moral certainties that characterised 19th century thought. But at the same time, he denied their foundational basis; indeed, he went further, in that he would at least on occasion suggest that an incorrect view of moral foundations would ultimately lead to awful consequences. As a matter of fact, one disaster, the Great War, happened in Conrad's lifetime, and though he wrote comparatively little about it it clearly influenced his work. Problems of morality, authority and meaning dogged 20th century thought from Nietszche to Beckett to Camus to Pinter, and affect all our political decisions from whether to try to prevent Iran developing nuclear capability down to whether kids wearing hoodies should be banned from shopping malls. In the abstract, can we (assuming 'we' can define 'ourselves' without begging questions) assemble sufficient moral authority and legitimacy to abrogate 'their' rights, while insisting on ours (to possess nuclear weapons, or to wear what we like without interference)? Conrad's monstrous suggestion is that faith that we can muster such authority is pervasive and corrosive, and he is prepared to make himself unpopular pointing it out.

The knitting machine

In *Nostromo*, Martin Decoud's suicide takes place amid great natural beauty.

> The dawn from behind the mountains put a gleam into his unwinking eyes. After a clear daybreak the sun appeared splen-

didly above the peaks of the range. The great gulf burst into a glitter all around the boat; and in this glory of merciless solitude the silence appeared again before him, stretched taut like a dark, thin string.

As Decoud falls from the boat, the sea's "glittering surface remained untroubled by the fall of his body." The world is indifferent to humanity, its suffering, its joys, its achievements. Conrad would certainly qualify recent calls from greens to 'save the planet': for Conrad the planet will go on, and on. Whether the planet can remain *humanly* habitable is a different, and perhaps pressing, question. Whether the Earth can remain a place of pleasure and beauty is one question more. But the planet will go on, without heeding our aesthetic judgements or political needs.

It is, on the face of it, an extraordinary myth that the world is there for our convenience. In different ways, Christians, neo-liberals and socialists all share this view of the world as ours, as a *resource*. Not all religions or ideologies hold that *prima facie* implausible line, but Conrad was not a Hermann Hesse figure who could find solace in Eastern thought. Conrad saw the world not as our property, or as one with us, but rather the massive and unregarding theatre of our puny endeavours. The sea is a classic symbol of the mighty, unrelenting world tossing tiny human societies back and forth, while Conrad also writes of the East and West winds in similar fashion as mighty kings "whose standard, naturally, is that of might alone."[1] But the image of our relation to the world that stands out in Conrad's writings is ironically not in a piece written for (immediate) publication, but rather in a letter to Cunninghame Graham.

There is a, — let us say, — a machine. It evolved itself (I am severely scientific) out of a chaos of scraps of iron and behold! — it knits. I am horrified at the horrible work and stand appalled. I feel it ought to embroider, — but it goes on knitting. You come and say: 'This is all right: It's only a question of the right kind of oil. Let us use this, — for instance, — celestial oil and the machine will embroider a most beautiful design in purple and gold.' Will it? Alas, no! You cannot by any special lubrication make embroidery with a knitting machine. And the most withering thought is that the infamous thing has made itself: made itself without thought, without conscience, without foresight, without eyes, without heart. It is a tragic accident, — and it has happened. You can't interfere with it. The last drop of bitterness is in the suspicion that you can't even smash it. In virtue of that truth one and

[1] In *The Mirror of the Sea*.

immortal which lurks in the force that made it spring into existence it is what it is, — and it is indestructible!

It knits us in and it knits us out. It has knitted time, space, pain, death, corruption, despair and all the illusions, — and nothing matters. I'll admit however that to look at the remorseless process is sometimes amusing.

The inevitability of the machine is, from a human perspective, contingent, not only unpredictable but also unrationalisable. Consider the gradual deconstruction of the mystery of James Wait in *The Nigger of the "Narcissus"*. He begins the novel portentously, as an intriguing conundrum. But as the voyage continues, and he argues with Donkin, Captain Allistoun and the evangelical Podmore, we end with an anticlimax: he is afraid of death. He unsettles the crew because they do not have his measure. He may, or may not, die. But he will die, sooner or later, and he is a disruptive element for the crew because he will not face that fact. What Ian Watt has called this "universal human reluctance" to face the unpleasant fact of an unregarding world is the subject of very much of Conrad's finest work.[2]

Understanding, or lack of it

Necessity becomes contingency: the apparent paradox happens because we cannot see the 'knitting machine' from an epistemologically helpful perspective. We have only our senses and our sciences, and our points of view are compromised by our preconceptions. As Razumov says to Haldin, we think "against" our families and cultures. The works of Conrad abound in misunderstandings, misreadings and inconsistent memories. *Victory, Almayer's Folly* or any one of a dozen books demonstrate the unreliability of a human being's epistemological position. Conrad dramatises uncertainty with his narratorial strategies, using unreliable reporters like Marlow and the teacher of English of *Under Western Eyes*, as well as setting them within framing stories narrated by still other, silent, unobtrusive commentators (Marlow's great moments in 'Heart of darkness' and *Lord Jim* are both narratives delivered to the 'narrator', who narrates Marlow's narration for us, the readers). Not only sense experience is unreliable; Conrad also indicts memory, reason and

[2]   Ian Watt, 'Conrad criticism and *The Nigger of the "Narcissus"*', in *Essays on Conrad*, Cambridge: Cambridge University Press, 2000, 64-84, at 78.

understanding. Even human sympathy is flawed, without the means of determining men's thoughts and motives.[3]

Conrad certainly wasn't a sceptic in the Cartesian sense, someone who doubts the existence of everything. He was of a practical bent, and scientifically well-informed.[4] The knitting machine can be described, and acts with a regularity that is presumably amenable to investigation. Though Conrad does not swallow science whole, he allows that laws of nature are lawlike and in principle discoverable. And though he plays with supernatural effects on occasion in his fiction, he is not a believer in the occult: "all my moral and intellectual being is penetrated by an invincible conviction that whatever falls under the dominion of our senses must be in nature and, however exceptional, cannot differ in its essence from all the other effects of the visible and tangible world of which we are a self-conscious part."[5]

But Conrad certainly opposed *faith* in science, the idea that science might provide the answers to all the serious questions we need to ask. In *The Secret Agent*, which we discuss in more detail in the next chapter, a plot is hatched by a "foreign power" to plant a terrorist bomb in order to prompt a crackdown on revolutionaries by the authorities. But what to blow up?

> You anarchists should make it clear that you are perfectly deter-
> mined to make a clean sweep of the whole social creation. But
> how to get the appallingly absurd notion into the heads of the
> middle classes so that there should be no mistake? That's the
> question. By directing your blows at something outside the ordi-
> nary passions of humanity is the answer. ... [There] is learning —
> science. Any imbecile that has got an income believes in that. He
> does not know why, but he believes it matters somehow. It is the
> sacro-sanct fetish. All the damned professors are radicals at
> heart. Let them know that their great panjandrum has got to go
> too, to make room for the Future of the Proletariat. ... Their indig-
> nation would be above suspicion, no material interests being
> openly at stake, and it will alarm every selfishness of the class
> which should be impressed. They believe that in some mysteri-
> ous way science is at the source of their material prosperity. ...
> [W]hat is one to say to an act of destructive ferocity so absurd as
> to be incomprehensible, inexplicable, almost unthinkable; in fact,

[3]   Cf. e.g. the discussion in John G. Peters, *Conrad and Impressionism*, Cambridge: Cambridge University Press, 2001, 123-134.

[4]   Ian Watt, '*Heart of Darkness* and nineteenth-century thought', in Harold Bloom (ed.), *Modern Critical Interpretations: Joseph Conrad's Heart of Darkness*, New York: Chelsea House, 1987, 77-89.

[5]   In the 'Author's note' to *The Shadow-Line*.

mad? ... But not every science will do. The attack must have all
the shocking senselessness of gratuitous blasphemy. Since
bombs are your means of expression, it would be really telling if
one could throw a bomb into pure mathematics. But that is
impossible. ... What do you think of having a go at astronomy?

Science is untouchable. No-one could possibly have a rational griev-
ance against it. People want to be protected against terrorist out-
rages, but the attack on science will directly affect no-one.
Nevertheless, it will be all the more deeply felt, an attack on what
Conrad feared was becoming the source of spiritual feeling in
Edwardian society.

To repeat: Conrad was not a sceptic about scientific thought. But
science is not the only form of understanding, and instrumental
value is not the only source of value. Many crude forms of politics
developed from perfectly respectable scientific theories—Darwinism
spawned the eugenics movement, for instance—and advances in
various technical fields also brought about a feeling that societies
could be seen as machines to be controlled and steered towards
particular ends.

There is a long history of allowing the *appearance* of scientific
knowledge to drive political and social thinking, as in the theories of
Cesare Lombroso, who thought that criminality could be deduced
from physiognomy;[6] his theories get an examination in *The Secret
Agent* (one apostle of terrorist violence concludes "Lombroso is an
ass"). In more modern times, the Bell curve and IQ testing have led to
unfortunate social divisions, while statistics-based surveillance
techniques, intended to create 'profiles' of individuals or groups,
can end up excluding large numbers of innocent people with the
'wrong' set of characteristics.[7] Someone who is near to the 'classic'
profile of a terrorist will be regarded with extra suspicion, even
though the probability of anyone of the classic profile (if there can be
such a thing) actually being a terrorist will be tiny, the numbers of
terrorists being so small.

That is not to say that science has *no* place in our deeper philosophical understanding. To take two examples, the development of the
philosophy of the human mind has depended for decades on discoveries in the neurosciences, and to a lesser extent on the engineering
progress made in artificial intelligence, while economic theory has

[6]   Stephen Jay Gould, *The Mismeasure of Man* (rev. ed.), New York: W.W.
       Norton, 1996.
[7]   David Lyon, *Surveillance After September 11*, Cambridge: Polity Press, 2003.

been boosted, and often contradicted, by the analysis of giant quantities of economic data that can now be performed thanks to the increasing availability of computing power and memory. Indeed, these two fields are now being combined in the fascinating new academic discipline of *neuroeconomics*, in which the role of the brain in our decision- and choice-making is investigated.[8] But that does not mean that neuroscientific investigation tells us all we want to know about our choice-making behaviour. Understanding that our choices as individuals are not always (or even not often) classically rational, but rather driven by a good deal of emotional processing as well, is clearly a vital insight — but it cannot tell us whether our choices are good ones in terms of our spiritual health, or of the health of our society.

Recent theories about the pursuit of happiness clearly add to the depth of our political discourse,[9] and have even trickled through into the policies of major parties in the United Kingdom at least,[10] but the temptation to use insights about the neural basis of happiness to promote a basic utilitarian philosophy[11] are deeply misguided. The important arguments for and against utilitarianism have little to do with the practicality or otherwise of developing an objective happiness-measuring system. A recent popularisation of the idea that snap decisions and first impressions are better than complex decision-making processes makes a number of good points,[12] but cannot be decisive until we have worked out, painstakingly and politically, what a 'good outcome' actually is.[13] Conrad's argument is not with science, but with the use of science to decide, or to de-politicise, properly political matters. The Catholic Church once foolishly politicised the question of whether the Earth orbited the sun. Today's errors tend to be of the opposite sort. Crime is a social matter, yet Lombroso's theory threatened to make it a scientific one; even now various schemes are under consideration in the United

[8]   Paul Glimcher, *Decisions, Uncertainty and the Brain: The Science of Neuroeconomics*, Cambridge, MA: MIT Press, 2003.

[9]   Richard Layard, *Happiness: Lessons From a New Science*, London: Allen Lane, 2005, Oliver James, Affluenza, London: Vermilion, 2007.

[10] David Cameron, speech of 20th July, 2006, http://www.conservatives.com/tile.do?def=news.story.page&obj_id=131047&speeches=1.

[11] Layard, *Happiness*, 111-125.

[12] Malcolm Gladwell, *Blink: The Power of Thinking Without Thinking*, London: Penguin, 2006.

[13] S. Alexander Haslam, 'I think, therefore I err?' *Scientific American Mind*, 18(2), April/May, 2007, 16-17.

Kingdom to try to identify criminals before they have committed a
crime, to 'protect society' (cf. the idea of the Pre-Crime Bureau in the
movie *Minority Report*). We have to beware the "insufferable, hopelessly dense sufficiency which nothing but the frequentation of
science can give to the dullness of common mortals."[14] The point is
that science's value depends on whole social structures underpinning
its practice and epistemology; it cannot be *self*-legitimising.

A related fetish is the privileging of fact over value, self-consciously 'practical' or 'businesslike' talk which has been influential
in Western thought for a long time, reaching its apotheosis with the
logical positivists, who believed that all knowledge is based either
directly on observation or on logical inference from it, and who
began their investigations round about the time of Conrad's death.[15]
In *Victory*, Heyst goes in search of facts, but in the end discovers that
all the important knowledge had fallen through the interstices. In
Lord Jim, the *Patna* inquiry wants the facts about the dereliction of
duty, but Marlow sneers "They wanted facts. Facts! They demanded
facts from him, as if facts could explain anything!" Facts are vital
inputs into our reasoning—they cannot be ignored, as Wait tries to
ignore them—but they should not determine the output, particularly when we are in the realm of moral reasoning. Indeed, they cannot determine the output, because each of us reasons in a different
way, brings different assumptions to bear and finds different things
significant: "facts, whatever their origin (and God only knows
where they come from), can be only tested by our own particular
suspicions."[16] This reflection is as pertinent now as when Conrad
was writing, when utilitarianism and positivism were still powerful
ideologies. Neither the Hayekian/Thatcherite neo-liberal doctrine
that competitive bidding markets should have a privileged role in
determining value, nor the New Labour view that bland target-
driven managerialism is an advance over deeply political discussions about what counts as a 'successful health outcome' (or whatever), can possibly be satisfactory except when they constitute part
of the reaction (as they both did in their initial implementations) to a
previous mistaken doctrine.[17]

[14]   Conrad's scathing remark about Ossipon, the scientific anarchist in *The
       Secret Agent*.
[15]   A.J. Ayer, *Language, Truth and Logic*, London: Victor Gollancz, 1936.
[16]   From *Victory*.
[17]   Kieron O'Hara, *After Blair: David Cameron and the Conservative Tradition*,
       Cambridge: Icon Books, 2007, 134-148, 173-210.

Conrad's only story of the Great War, 'The tale', is a fable about a naval commanding officer who, while sheltering in a cove during a thick fog, discovers a supposedly neutral ship in the same cove. He investigates, and convinces himself to his own satisfaction that the second vessel has in fact been provisioning enemy submarines. He decides to test his theory: he plots the 'neutral' captain a course that will take his ship through treacherous rocks. If the captain is guilty, then he would know the region and avoid the rocks as he made his escape. But the captain follows the course and his ship is lost with all hands. Was it merely that he did not know the coast well enough? Or was he innocent after all? Was the officer guilty of unwarranted slaughter of his fellow seamen? Or was he really doling out justice — stern justice, but justice nonetheless? He cannot know.

Life "is so much like a dream," says Decoud in *Nostromo*. But though we are surrounded, and indeed motivated by illusion, we must not allow ourselves to ignore fact, to succumb to fatalism. Death, for instance, is a fact, but whether a death is ignoble or inspiring is not something that can be determined by a scientific investigation. In the early story 'Karain', a story of the South Seas, Conrad makes it clear that it is not the facts of the matter that carry value, but the experience of them — "the illusions as restless as men; of the illusions faithful, faithless; of the illusions that give joy, that give sorrow, that give pain, that give peace; of the invincible illusions that can make life and death appear serene, inspiring, tormented, or ignoble." At the end, the framing narrative returns to the bustle of a crowded and realistically-described London. But still:

> 'Yes; I see it [the London street, with its traffic and people],' said Jackson, slowly. 'It is there; it pants, it runs, it rolls; it is strong and alive; it would smash you if you didn't look out; but I'll be hanged if it is yet as real to me as … as the other thing … say, Karain's story.'[18]

The narrator remarks that "decidedly, [Jackson] had been too long away from home." But Jackson, and Conrad through him, is not saying that reality is illusory. The great knitting machine is not illusory. It is *significance* that is an illusion.

The myth of progress

Significance is often determined for people by abstract theory. Jim's ideal of himself determined how he should view his actions, and his

[18]   Conrad's ellipses.

ideal was a good one — until it outstripped his bravery. As her husband builds up the silver mine to ensure the "prosperity and peace of Sulaco", Mrs Gould "watched his abstraction with dread." "A man haunted by a fixed idea is insane. He is dangerous even if that idea is an idea of justice; for may he not bring the heaven down pitilessly upon a loved head?" The grosser pretensions of abstract ideas have been clear ever since Plato's *Euthyphro*, but they still hold sway.

'Karain' is a story about an ancient and horribly modern phenomenon: honour killing. Karain is a Malay chief haunted by the ghost of his friend Pata Matara. Matara's sister married a Dutchman, bringing dishonour on her family, and Matara, taking Karain, sets out to expunge the dishonour by killing them. The quest takes years, during which Karain develops an idea of the sister, and falls in love with the person he has constructed; he talks to her at night, and she is his constant companion as he travels around unfamiliar islands with Matara always searching. When they finally find the sister and the Dutchman, Matara prepares to kill them, but before he can Karain shoots him. Two ideals come into conflict: does Karain allow his friend to avenge the dishonour, or does he betray their friendship? Karain chooses humanity over the absolute.

The concrete and actual has a clear epistemological precedence over the potential and abstract.[19] We might not be able to understand everything about the world, but we can certainly judge it; the point of a philosophical theory, on the other hand, is to fit the facts into a framework. That is all very well, until we allow the theory to ground the facts' significance. Conrad argued that it was better to have a few simple ideals than a complex set of theories and prescriptions; theories persist horribly in the environment, like pollution. They are not biodegradable. Marxism, all of whose major predictions proved false almost before the ink with which they were transcribed was dry, continued to exert an extraordinary hold over very many very clever people for a century and more.

The great hope of mankind is to improve its lot. Progress is a matter of theory and mensuration; it implies a yardstick against which we must place ourselves. There is nothing wrong with progress: central heating and CD players are nice. But there is danger when failure to progress is put down to failure not of a theory, but of the human

[19]   Kieron O'Hara, *After Blair*, 59-155.

beings it purports to measure to live up to it. Those who have not progressed are stigmatised as 'backward'.[20]

Such thoughts have given rationality a bad name — a name that it does not deserve. Rationality, science and engineering are vital for humankind and its future. But they should not be mixed up with a notion of 'progress' which (a) is a *subjective* description of a set of situations through time, and (b) is certainly not inevitable, be we ever so scientific. Theories can prove false, or unsuited for particular contexts; if we act on the theory rather than the facts, we can do the wrong thing. As Heyst ponders, "Action — the first thought, or perhaps the first impulse, on earth! The barbed hook, baited with the illusion of progress, to bring out of the lightless void the shoals of unnumbered generations!" Is there a better description, for example, of the ill-fated scheme to bring democracy to the undoubtedly oppressed people of Iraq?[21]

In fact, Conrad had already worried about unrealistic American idealism in his own time. Woodrow Wilson's positive vision of the post-Great War settlement left him very cold indeed. In a letter of 1919, he complained of "an awful sense of unreality in all this babel of League of Nations and Reconstruction and production of Commodities and Industrial arrangements, while Fisher prattles solemnly about education and Conciliation Boards are being set up to bring about a union of hearts while the bare conciliation of interests is obviously impossible. It is like people laying out a tennis court on a ground that is already moving under their feet." Hitler came to power fourteen years later.[22]

"An incorrigible mankind hardens its heart in the progress of its own perfectability", he wrote in *The Mirror of the Sea*. In his day, perfection was believed to stem from a Darwinistic interpretation of the survival of the fittest. Fitness is good, so the survival of the fittest is

[20] The term 'developing world', which I have used elsewhere in this book, is often criticised as implying failure, or at least tardiness, in comparison with the 'developed world'. I do not support this implication; I use the terms solely because they are reasonably well-understood, and in more common use than other terms. Economists and geographers are beginning to use technical-sounding jargon such as 'less developed country' and 'less economically developed country' (LDC and LEDC), while many political writers talk of 'The North' and 'The South', or 'The West' and 'The Rest'.

[21] See the dialectic in Fukuyama's work, between Francis Fukuyama, *The End of History and the Last Man*, New York: Free Press, 1992, and *After the Neocons: America at the Crossroads*, London: Profile Books, 2006.

[22] Ironically, it was a Polish government which first defied the League of Nations, annexing Vilnius (Wilno) in 1920.

good — but it does not follow that the elimination of the unfit is also good. Darwin never made socio-political deductions but many thinkers (notably Herbert Spencer) were deeply optimistic about the possibilities for progress and the perfection of mankind on Darwinian grounds. That optimism fed through into theories of racial superiority, and indirectly the colonial rape.[23] The endpoint of the application of such theories, for Conrad, was Kurtz (see Chapter Two).

Progress is relative to theories, and we do not understand the world, or ourselves, or each other, well enough to produce theories good enough to define progress objectively for all contexts. Progress can be central heating, or food on the table, or women's rights, or a decline in crime, or any of the wonders of 21st century life. But at the same time, progress is climate change, loss of biodiversity and 'the end of the wild',[24] it is boy soldiers with AK-47s and blood diamonds. It is the beautiful, glistening towers at the centre of a city, and the slums and shanty towns at its edge. It is an instantaneous global information system, and the attack on the World Trade Center in 2001.[25]

Pessimism

Theories and belief systems are not universal, nor universally interpreted in the same way. They cannot lead us effectively; they cannot ensure progress even on their own terms. They mislead even the best of us. Especially the best of us (the phenomenal Kurtz).

> Consciously or unconsciously, men are proud of their firmness, steadfastness of purpose, directness of aim. They go straight towards their desire, to the accomplishment of virtue — sometimes of crime — in an uplifting persuasion of their firmness. They walk the road of life, the road fenced in by their tastes, prejudices, disdains or enthusiasms, generally honest, invariably stupid, and are proud of never losing their way. If they do stop, it is to look for a moment over the hedges that make them safe, to look at the misty valleys, at the distant peaks, at cliffs and morasses, at the dark forests and the hazy plains where other human beings grope their days painfully away, stumbling over the bones of the wise, over the unburied remains of their prede-

[23] Watt, '*Heart of Darkness* and nineteenth-century thought', 80-82.
[24] Stephen M. Meyer, *The End of the Wild*, Somerville, MA: Boston Review, 2006.
[25] John Gray, *Al Qaeda and What it Means to be Modern*, London: Faber & Faber, 2003.

cessors who died alone, in gloom or in sunshine, half-way from anywhere. The man of purpose does not understand, and goes on, full of contempt. He never loses his way. He knows where he is going and what he wants. Travelling on, he achieves great length without any breadth, and battered, besmirched, and weary, he touches the goal at last; he grasps the reward of his perseverance, of his virtue, of his healthy optimism: an untruthful tombstone over a dark and soon forgotten grave.[26]

In the context of ideas of progress, we have to be pessimistic; the world will never match our hopes and plans, and hopes lead to disappointment. After Willems' treachery in *An Outcast of the Islands*, Almayer's anger comes out in a drunken rant that stands for all the frustrations of people with hopes, ideas and schemes.

> Here I am! Done harm to nobody, lived an honest life … and a scoundrel like that is born in Rotterdam or some such damn'd place at the other end of the world somewhere, travels out here, robs his employer, runs away from his wife, and ruins me and my Nina — he ruined me, I tell you — and gets himself shot at last by a poor miserable savage, that knows nothing at all about him really. Where's the sense of all this? Where's your providence? Where's the good for anybody in all this? The world's a swindle! A swindle! Why should I suffer? What have I done to be treated so?[27]

The epigraph to *Almayer's Folly* is a quote from the Swiss philosopher Amiel which universalises Almayer's predicament: "which of us has not had his promised land, his day of ecstasy, and his end in exile?" Ian Watt argued that Almayer is merely being selfish, and frustrated because he has not become rich; his petulance rules him out as a universal figure.[28] But do we have to accept that negative judgement? Mayn't Almayer's hopes — which were for his daughter, of course, as well as for himself — make him a figure that consumerist individualists of the 21st century can recognise? He wanted to leave the South Seas and spend his retirement in comfort in Europe with Nina. He had a notion of progress, and he had an idea of a better place, ideas that Nina could not share. In the end he had to watch her sail away with her Balinese lover. His pathetic attempt to erase her memory — filling in her footprints on the beach with sand — is doomed. Our schemes fail, and we have to watch; does the reaction

[26] From *An Outcast of the Islands*.
[27] Conrad's ellipsis.
[28] Ian Watt, '*Almayer's Folly*: introduction', in *Essays on Conrad*, 20-63, at 57.

have to be temperate to be properly universal? Almayer is certainly not a noble figure — but which of us is?

Making meaning

The world has no ultimate meaning, argues Conrad. It knits us out and in and we can't change it except on the margins. But that something has no meaning in a foundational sense does not mean that things do not *have* meaning. We give them meaning, contingently, locally; Chapters Five to Seven above discussed three key ways in which meaning is given to social relations.

We know that no absolutes exist to underpin our experience, and Conrad argues — particularly in 'Heart of darkness' — that assuming otherwise will cause harm, because one will be tempted to apply one's principles too far, as did Kurtz. "Principles won't do," says Marlow. "Acquisitions, clothes, pretty rags — rags that would fly off at the first good shake. No; you want a deliberate belief." Conrad certainly shares beliefs in broadly Western moral principles; he is neither a hedonist, nor a moral sceptic. But he does not assume that his principles are self-evident, or that they should be imposed on other peoples (the colonial project). As we argued in Chapter Two, he is not interested in the principles of 'natives', but he does not think his own principles superior to theirs.

Work and community are both ways in which we forge relationships with others, and find ourselves with moral obligations — reasons to live. We do not move blindly; this is not Samuel Beckett's "I can't go on, I'll go on." Moral isolation is not the condition of mankind, but when it occurs it leads, in Conrad's work, to tragedy. One can be isolated by actions in one's past (Jim, Willems, Falk, Razumov), by circumstances (Yanko Goorall, Almayer), by an inability to communicate (the Goulds, or the Verlocs in *The Secret Agent*) or by one's principles (Heyst, Kurtz), but however one loses moral connection to others, the result is disastrous.

Moral schemes should be simple, widely applicable. One has friends, family, workmates — one should be faithful to them. The "temporal world rests on a few very simple ideas; so simple that they must be as old as the hills."[29] And sometimes we simply cannot plan, or consult our ideal schemes. Sometimes the extreme event occurs, and our actions 'happen' to us, and our lives are changed. Under pressure from such events, and from our ties of community and

[29] From *A Personal Record*.

work, we find out what we are. We can understand and control a little part of the world, where life is tolerable. We provide its value.

An act of symbolism – the creation of a meaning for some object – cannot simply happen willy-nilly.

> Can I then not use words to mean what I like? – Look at the door of your room, utter a sequence of random sounds and mean by them a description of that door.

> 'Say "a b c d" and mean: the weather is fine.'[30]

But it can happen relatively simply and in unexpected ways. After killing his friend Matara, Karain believes he is haunted by his ghost. He becomes fearful, and ceases to lead his people, which worries the white gun-runners who supply him and his tribe with weapons. He pleads with them to take him away from his lands.

> You know us. You have lived with us. Why? – we cannot know; but you understand our sorrows and our thoughts. You have lived with my people, and you understand our desires and our fears. With you I will go. To your land – to your people. To your people, who live in unbelief; to whom day is day, and night is night – nothing more, because you understand all things seen, and despise all else! To your land of unbelief, where the dead do not speak, where every man is wise, and alone – and at peace! ...

> Take me with you ... Or else give me some of your strength – of your unbelief ... A charm! ...[31]

One of the gun-runners has a brainwave, and with solemn ceremony, presents Karain with a sixpence, with the image of the Great Queen, "the most powerful thing the white men know." The 'charm' works, and the ghost disappears.

Meanings can be made, but not simply. And it is unjustified optimism to presume that ties of work and community that virtually all people have will cause them to behave loyally and morally; we know from observation that this is not true. The world is not like that, and we should structure our society and institutions to respect the fact, as Conrad wrote to his socialist friend Cunninghame Graham in 1897.

> You want from men faith, honour, fidelity to truth in themselves and others. You want them to have all this, to show it every day, to make out of these words their rules of life. The respectable classes which suspect you of such pernicious longings lock you

[30] Ludwig Wittgenstein, *Zettel* (2nd edition, G.E.M. Anscombe & G.H. von Wright, eds., G.E.M. Anscombe, trans.), Oxford: Basil Blackwell, 1981, §§5-6.
[31] All but the first ellipsis Conrad's.

up and would just as soon have you shot, — because your personality counts and you cannot deny that you are a dangerous man.
What makes you dangerous is your unwarrantable belief that
your desire may be realised. This is the only point of difference
between us. I do not believe. And if I desire the very same things
no one cares. Consequently I am not likely to be locked up or
shot.

The aim of government should not be to allow the individual as free
rein as possible — that will be chaos, and damaging to the very bonds
of community that are required to keep us together. Kurtz is the endpoint of that political project. Rather, the value of restraint should be
asserted. How, asks Marlow of his friends, could they understand
Kurtz?

How could you — with solid pavement under your feet, surrounded by kind neighbours ready to cheer you or to fall on you,
stepping delicately between the butcher and the policeman, in
the holy terror of scandal and gallows and lunatic asylums — how
can you imagine what particular region of the first ages a man's
untrammelled feet may take him into by the way of solitude —
utter solitude without a policeman — by way of silence — utter
silence, where no warning voice of a kind neighbour can be heard
whispering of public opinion? These little things make all the
great difference.

Razumov, after he has betrayed Haldin, writes down the ways in
which he believes we can legitimately gain understanding and
change.

History, not Theory.
Patriotism, not Internationalism.
Evolution, not Revolution.
Direction, not Destruction.
Unity, not Disruption.

We do not have the moral authority, or the knowledge, to impose
change. We cannot anticipate events. We do not understand others'
desires or beliefs. We cannot generate authority for positive change
based on abstract theories. What we can do is foster change, direct
evolution, maintain the community — and we do not pick and choose
our communities, by and large. Our solidarity is with our fellows,
not the whole of mankind.

Conrad's descriptions of societies are conservative ones, but not
unrealistic. For instance, in *The Nigger of the "Narcissus"*, one can take
umbrage at his description of Donkin and his rabble-rousing, but
equally the narrative gives a pretty unvarnished view of the hard-

ships and small rewards available for the lower class crewmen, while Captain Allistoun, we gather, won't get a command because of his lack of connections. Unremarkable characters gain strength, and become admirable, in the performance of their roles within the workplace and the community.[32]

What to do

One reaction to this is fatalism, to let what will be, be. Should scepticism and pessimism result in paralysis? Conrad believed not.

> Babalatchi's fatalism gave him only an insignificant relief in his suspense, because no fatalism can kill the thought of the future, the desire of success, the pain of waiting for the disclosure of the immutable decrees of Heaven. Fatalism is born of the fear of failure, for we all believe that we carry success in our own hands, and we suspect our hands are weak.[33]

We must act, and we must plan. But we cannot expect success, we should not expect to improve the lot of others (even if that is what we want to do), and we shouldn't howl at the moon if we fail. Our hands *are* weak, though we are wrong to believe that we carry our success. To take our pessimism as far as fatalism is to commit what Cedric Watts calls the antipathetic fallacy, which is to assume that because we know very little, and that the world is indifferent to our desires, everything will go wrong.[34] This does not follow from Conrad's scepticism and pessimism. Although action gives "the illusion of a mastered destiny,"[35] that does not mean that things will turn out opposite to our intentions. We cannot assume that things will go right, that progress will be made, or, if it is, that we shall enjoy it; but equally we cannot avoid doing *something*. As soon as we have any relationships with anyone, we are sucked into a world of obligation and action, as Heyst (in *Victory*) and Peyrol (in *The Rover*) discover. Both men die at the end of their respective novels, but only the former has failed.

Conrad was deeply pessimistic (his uncle addressed him as "my dear pessimist" in a letter of November 1891), but in his stronger moments he would hold out against it. In his essay 'Books', he argues that he is not claiming "the freedom of moral Nihilism." "To

[32] Watt, 'Conrad criticism and *The Nigger of the "Narcissus"'*, 82.
[33] From *An Outcast of the Islands*.
[34] Cedric Watts, Conrad's *'Heart of Darkness': A Critical and Contextual Discussion*, Milan: Mursia International, 1977, 18-21.
[35] From 'Autocracy and war'.

be hopeful in an artistic sense it is not necessary to think that the world is good. It is enough to believe that there is no impossibility of its being made so." "What one feels so hopelessly barren in declared pessimism is just its arrogance." To think that everything will turn out badly is just as unjustified an idea as that everything will turn out well.

Conrad was alive to this sort of charge, and *Under Western Eyes* argues precisely that Russia was too far gone to carry on, and his 'Author's note' to the novel, written after the Russian revolution, shows he was certainly aware that something had to give. In 'Autocracy and war', he had written, of Russia's defeat in battle by the resurgent Japanese:

> And above it all — unaccountably persistent — the decrepit, old, hundred years old, spectre of Russia's might still faces Europe from across the teeming graves of Russian people. This dreaded and strange apparition, bristling with bayonets, armed with chains, hung over with holy images; that something not of this world, partaking of a ravenous ghoul, of a blind Djinn grown up from a cloud, and of the Old Man of the Sea, still faces us with its old stupidity, with its strange mystical arrogance, stamping its shadowy feet upon the gravestone of autocracy, already cracked beyond repair by the torpedoes of Togo and the guns of Oyama, already heaving in the blood-soaked ground with the first stirrings of a resurrection.

> Never before had the Western world the opportunity to look so deep into the black abyss which separates a soulless autocracy posing as, and even believing itself to be, the arbiter of Europe, from the benighted, starved souls of its people. This is the real object-lesson of this war, its unforgettable information.

He concluded, correctly, that "the downfall of Russia's might is unavoidable", and, worse, "For the autocracy of Holy Russia the only conceivable self-reform is — suicide." He also made a serious effort to understand the revolutionary urge, and *Under Western Eyes* makes a stab at explaining why the legitimate desire to end tyranny led to "imbecile and atrocious" Utopianism. Sometimes, actions have to occur that are far-reaching in their effects, at both the micro and macro scale. Karain was faced with the choice of killing his friend or watching the death of the real-world counterpart of his reified ideal. Poland's rebellions against the Russian yoke were justified, even though hopeless.

Behaving in a moral way will provide a moral compass, to help avoid the docility of conservatism. In *Victory*, Heyst has sworn not to act, but he must — sworn to look on, but he cannot. He cannot avoid ties, and with real ties, openly entered into, come obligations for action. Conservatism, allied to a plain morality, will not lead to inaction. "All ambitions are lawful except those which climb upward on the miseries or credulities of mankind."

> The sight of human affairs deserves admiration and pity. They are worthy of respect, too. And he is not insensible who pays them the undemonstrative tribute of a sigh which is not a sob, and of a smile which is not a grin. Resignation, not mystic, not detached, but resignation open-eyed, conscious, and informed by love, is the only one of our feelings for which it is impossible to become a sham.
>
> Not that I think resignation the last word of wisdom. I am too much the creature of my time for that. But I think the proper wisdom is to will what the gods will without, perhaps, being certain what their will is — or even if they have a will of their own. And in this matter of life and art it is not the Why that matters so much to our happiness as the How. ...
>
> Those who read me know my conviction that the world, the temporal world, rests on a few very simple ideas; so simple that they must be as old as the hills. It rests notably, among others, on the idea of Fidelity. At a time when nothing which is not revolutionary in some way or other can expect to attract much attention I have not been revolutionary in my writings. The revolutionary spirit is mighty convenient in this, that it frees one from all scruples as regards ideas. Its hard, absolute optimism is repulsive to my mind by the menace of fanaticism and intolerance it contains. ... All claim to special righteousness awakens in me that scorn and anger from which a philosophical mind should be free.[36]

Nihilism

So work, community and "a few very simple ideas" bring Conrad to a conservative position, respecting society, promoting tolerance, avoiding claims to righteousness. But has he been too sweeping? Do his scepticism and rejection of a unique and authoritative narrative of events, leave the door open to a kind of nihilism? "The special place of Joseph Conrad in English Literature," it has been claimed, "lies in the fact that in him the nihilism covertly dominant in modern culture is brought to the surface and shown for what it is."[37] Is there

---

[36] From 'A familar preface' to A Personal Record.
[37] J. Hillis Miller, *Poets of Reality: Six Twentieth-Century Writers*, New York: Atheneum, 1974, 5.

in’s ideas to dissuade those of a revolutionary bent
from pressing their case in ways designed to disrupt and destroy
community, and problematising simple ideas?

This is certainly a pressing issue on Conrad's 150th birthday. He
was never a moral relativist, and certainly not a nihilist, but he is
now seen as a key figure in the subversion of the moral scheme to
which he adhered. He was aware of the risk that a moral code without foundations would be disregarded; many a preacher has
exploited the sad psychological truth that fear of hellfire is a more
persuasive argument than the obvious social benefits of moral
behaviour. He saw the foundational project as dangerous, but many
parts of Western society, especially the guardians and curators of
our culture, have descended into a relativism about morality that
makes it very hard for them to respond to serious threats from violent zealots. Revolutionary violence is a part of our age. And that is
something about which Conrad had a lot to say.

Chapter Nine

Terror

The Secret Agent

Conrad's novel *The Secret Agent* — the only one of his major works which we have not yet discussed in detail — is an odd phenomenon, a novel that "is now regarded as his consummate achievement in the art of fiction", despite the fact that "if there is one point on which critics agree, it is that the novel does not offer a serious intellectual challenge."[1] This curious state of affairs is not, of course, tenable. The cause, I think, is Conrad's use of irony, the deliberate undercutting of what a particular statement purports to say. Conrad was always an ironist, but in *The Secret Agent* he lays it on with a trowel. This has two effects. First of all, the book is very funny even (or especially) when it is most disturbing or tragic; perhaps this means it is taken less seriously. It is perceived by some as unnecessarily flippant.[2] And secondly, the book is not about what it purports to be about, the plans and schemes of a group of anarchist spies in 19th century London. In fact, as a discussion of anarchism and revolution, *The Secret Agent* is less than adequate.

The story centres around Adolf Verloc, an indolent middle-aged man running a series of more or less interrelated lives in a shabby, dark, polluted London. His business is a shop selling pornography. He is at the centre of a small ring of anarchists that meets to plot and intrigue. He is also a triple agent, reporting to a foreign embassy on the anarchists' doings, and to the London police force. Domestically, his situation is hardly blissful but serviceable for his needs. His wife Winnie has no feeling for him, and married him to provide a home for her elderly mother and mentally retarded brother Stevie. Verloc

[1]   Jacques Berthoud, '*The Secret Agent*', in J.H. Stape (ed.), *The Cambridge Companion to Joseph Conrad*, Cambridge: Cambridge University Press, 1996, 100-121, at 100 & 103.

[2]   E.g. Jocelyn Baines, *Joseph Conrad: A Critical Biography*, Harmondsworth: Penguin, 1971, at 396-408.

has no inkling that Winnie has this contractual view of their marriage, doling out joyless sex for him when he wants or needs it. Verloc is ordered by Mr Vladimir of the foreign power to commit a terrorist outrage at the Greenwich Observatory (discussed in Chapter Eight, above), in order to provoke a clampdown on the anarchists by the London police. To this end, he recruits Stevie, whose compassion for the oppressed is boundless, to carry the bomb — yet Stevie slips and falls, and the bomb detonates, killing him and doing no other damage. Verloc avoids telling Winnie of the tragedy, but she of course finds out, and takes a terrible revenge, stabbing him as he lies complacently on the settee.

Certainly a melodramatic plot — though based on fact. An attempt to blow up the Observatory in 1894 did result in the death of one Martial Bourdin, "half an idiot", who was carrying a bomb on the orders of a would-be mastermind. Even the melodrama of the story is the product, not of Conrad's following the spy genre, but of the characters' own melodramatic behaviour; one way of seeing *The Secret Agent* is as a realistic book about melodramatic people. But the main thing to note is that the book, despite appearances, is much more about the society that hosts anarchist terror, than the terror, or the ideology, itself.

For this, we have Conrad's own statements in a series of letters written about the novel. To John Galsworthy, in 1906, he wrote:

> The point of *treatment* You raise I have already considered. In such a tale one is likely to be misunderstood. After all you must not take it too seriously. The whole thing is superficial and it is but *a tale*. I had no idea to consider Anarchism politically — or to treat it seriously in its philosophical aspect: as a manifestation of human nature in its discontent and imbecility. The general reflections whether right or wrong are not meant as bolts. You can't say I *hurl* them in any sense. ... They are — if anything — mere digs at the people in the tale. As to attacking anarchism as a form of humanitarian enthusiasm or intellectual despair or social atheism that — if it were worth doing — would be the work for a more vigorous hand and for a mind more robust, and perhaps more honest than mine.

In 1907 he remarked to Cunninghame Graham "But I don't think that I've been satirizing the revolutionary world. All these people are not revolutionaries — they are shams."

The goodies and the baddies

The shams are clearly shams, which is one reason why the book has had such a disjointed reception; they do not stand as convincing revolutionaries, unlike those in *Under Western Eyes*. Verloc is corpulent: "Undemonstrative and burly in a fat pig style". As Mr Vladimir taunts him, "You — a member of a starving proletariat — never!" He is also idle.

> He was in a manner devoted to it with a sort of inert fanaticism, or perhaps rather with a fanatical inertness. Born of industrious parents for a life of toil, he had embraced indolence from an impulse as profound, as inexplicable and as imperious as the impulse which directs a man's preference for one particular woman in a given thousand. He was too lazy even for a mere demagogue, for a workman orator, for a leader of labour. It was too much trouble. He required a more perfect form of ease; or it might have been that he was the victim of a philosophical unbelief in the effectiveness of every human effort. Such a form of indolence requires, implies, a certain amount of intelligence. Mr Verloc was not devoid of intelligence — and at the notion of a menaced social order he would perhaps have winked to himself if there had not been an effort to make in that sign of scepticism. His big, prominent eyes were not well adapted to winking. They were rather of the sort that closes solemnly in slumber with majestic effect.

He has no beliefs, no country (although he is a "natural born British subject" with a French father, he only lives in London because ordered to by his masters), no skills, no work — he remains unformed by the characteristic influences discussed above in Chapters Six and Seven. He is a fraud, and as Mr Vladimir, a man of wit and talent, realises, so is his whole set-up. Verloc's original employer, Baron Stott-Wartenheim, only ever referred to Verloc as Δ — a ludicrous extra-secret designation for a man who "looked uncommonly like a master plumber come to present his bill." The Baron "had the social revolution on the brain", and "was fated to be the victim of the first humbugging rascal that came along, thought Mr Vladimir, smiling vaguely at Mr Verloc."

Four anarchists visit Verloc regularly; one, the Professor, we will discuss later in the chapter. Michaelis is an unworldly figure, "so far from pessimism that he saw already the end of all private property coming along logically, unavoidably, by the mere development of its inherent viciousness." Here is one type of social reformer, someone who sees his hopes and compassion reflected in the world, someone who thinks that all will turn out nicely — and fools himself into thinking that "cold reason" is the "basis of his optimism." He is an intellectual extension of the compassionate and emotional Stevie. The third anarchist, Ossipon, fancies a scientific rather than logical justification for anarchism.

Yundt is another type, a self-described terrorist. His contribution to the novel is to outline the rationale of the suicide bomber, some three quarters of a century before the civil wars in Lebanon and Sri Lanka led to the introduction and honing of the technique in the modern age.

> 'I have always dreamed,' he mouthed fiercely, 'of a band of men absolute in their resolve to discard all scruples in the choice of means, strong enough to give themselves frankly the name of destroyers, and free from the taint of that resigned pessimism which rots the world. No pity for anything on earth, including themselves — and death — enlisted for good and all in the service of humanity — that's what I would have liked to see. ... And I could never get as many as three such men together.'

But Verloc's group is no threat to society.

> In the light of Mr Vladimir's philosophy of bomb throwing they appeared hopelessly futile. The part of Mr Verloc in revolutionary politics having been to observe, he could not all at once, either in his own home or in larger assemblies, take the initiative of action. ... [H]e asked himself scornfully what else could have been expected from such a lot, this Karl Yundt, this Michaelis — this Ossipon.

> ... A lazy lot — this Karl Yundt, nursed by a blear eyed old woman, a woman he had years ago enticed away from a friend, and afterwards had tried more than once to shake off into the gutter. Jolly lucky for Yundt that she had persisted in coming up time after time, or else there would have been no one now to help him out of the 'bus by the Green Park railings, where that spectre took its constitutional crawl every fine morning. When that indomitable snarling old witch died the swaggering spectre would have to vanish too — there would be an end to fiery Karl Yundt. And Mr Verloc's morality was offended also by the optimism of Michaelis, annexed by his wealthy old lady, who had taken lately to sending him to a cottage she had in the country. The ex-prisoner could moon about the shady lanes for days together in a delicious and humanitarian idleness. As to Ossipon, that beggar was sure to want for nothing as long as there were silly girls with savings bank books in the world. And Mr Verloc, temperamentally identical with his associates, drew fine distinctions in his mind on the strength of insignificant differences. He

drew them with a certain complacency, because the instinct of conventional respectability was strong within him, being only overcome by his dislike of all kinds of recognised labour — a temperamental defect which he shared with a large proportion of revolutionary reformers of a given social state. For obviously one does not revolt against the advantages and opportunities of that state, but against the price which must be paid for the same in the coin of accepted morality, self-restraint and toil. The majority of revolutionists are the enemies of discipline and fatigue mostly. There are natures too, to whose sense of justice the price exacted looms up monstrously enormous, odious, oppressive, worrying, humiliating, extortionate, intolerable. Those are the fanatics. The remaining portion of social rebels is accounted for by vanity, the mother of all noble and vile illusions, the companion of poets, reformers, charlatans, prophets, and incendiaries.

All the would-be terrorists suffer the lack of the major determinants of character discussed earlier. They do not work. They are exiled and indeed have rejected their countries. They have not developed ties with other human beings that go beyond the cynical and contractual (Verloc believes that his wife Winnie loves him, but she does not; he believes that he loves her, but in fact is using her).

So far, *The Secret Agent* seems to be a critique of terrorism and revolutionaries, but soon enough we are introduced to the law-enforcement agencies, equally unedifying. Chief Inspector Heat is charged with investigating the bomb outrage. He is comfortable with catching ordinary criminals "Thieving was not a sheer absurdity. ... [H]e could understand the mind of a burglar, because, as a matter of fact, the mind and the instincts of a burglar are of the same kind as the mind and the instincts of a police officer. Both recognise the same conventions, and have a working knowledge of each other's methods and of the routine in their respective trades." Anarchists and rebels, in contrast, confuse him. Evidence is discovered connecting Verloc with the explosion, but Heat wishes to charge the innocent Michaelis with the crime because Verloc is one of his informers. However, his superior, the Assistant Commissioner, won't let him do that, and takes Heat off the case. But even he is not driven by respect for truth, justice or procedure. Rather, his problem is his wife, who is a patron of Michaelis. "Damn it! If that infernal Heat has his way the fellow'll die in prison smothered in his fat, and she'll never forgive me."

The Secret Agent fits exactly the form of a standard piece of crime fiction: a villain commits, or attempts to commit a crime, a disinterested and legitimate investigator identifies the perpetrator, ensuring that justice is done and the moral fabric, rent by the original crime, is restored by the process. That does all happen in the novel. But the irony subverts all of the details, and we are not left with any confidence in the restoration of order. The villain, Verloc, does attempt a crime, but it is neither his idea nor his execution. The investigators of the CID do identify Verloc, although Heat hopes to blame Michaelis. Retributive justice is indeed done; though the police are willing to let Verloc go, he is killed by his wife Winnie. Winnie herself, having taken the law into her own hands, commits suicide. But can we really, in the face of all these self-interested actions with their perverse consequences, have any kind of confidence in the moral fabric?[3]

Complicity

Just as al-Qaeda thrives on and exploits the globalisation that it pretends to oppose,[4] and just as Vladimir's plan uses science (chemistry) to attack science at Greenwich, subversion needs the solid substrate of the society it affects to despise. As Michaelis puts it, "Capitalism has made socialism, and the laws made by capitalism for the protection of property are responsible for anarchism."

The society that nurtured the Verloc affair, in Conrad's view, was in a mess. The characteristic virtue that Conrad thought essential, the big lesson that he had learned from his twenty years at sea, was fidelity, but there is no faith in *The Secret Agent*. No-one shows loyalty to anyone, except Winnie and her mother to Stevie. Of the anarchists, only Michaelis is at all sympathetic. Those attacking society are not part of it, and have turned their back upon it, although they have no better ideas. Those defending it have become so focused upon the defence that they pursue it no matter what the cost to the society they nominally defend. The ignoble state of affairs described in the novel is what is left. The lesson in 2007, as our own ancient liberties are eroded in order to meet a similarly stated yet equally nebulous threat, is quite clear.

That the symbiosis between terror and counter-terror is not merely political was argued by Conrad in 'An anarchist', the story of Paul, an innocent man, sentenced to penal servitude for drunkenly espousing anarchism. Having escaped (and murdered his fellow

[3]   Berthoud, '*The Secret Agent*', 107-108.
[4]   John Gray, *Al Qaeda and What it Means to be Modern*, London: Faber & Faber, 2003, Olivier Roy, *Globalized Islam: The Search for a New Ummah*, New York: Columbia University Press, 2004.

accused, from revenge), he is effectively kept a prisoner on the estate of a classic 'material interest', B.O.S. Ltd., a giant food company "whose nourishment is offered to you not only highly concentrated, but already half-digested." The manager of the B.O.S. estate fulminates against Paul to the narrator.

'I am perfectly willing to take it that he has done nothing worse than to stick a knife into somebody — French fashion, don't you know. But that subversive sanguinary rot of doing away with all law and order in the world makes my blood boil. It's simply cutting the ground from under the feet of every decent, respectable, hard-working person. I tell you that the consciences of people who have them, like you or I, must be protected in some way; or else the first low scoundrel that came along would in every respect be just as good as myself. Wouldn't he now? And that's absurd!'

He glared at me. I nodded slightly and murmured that doubtless there was much subtle truth in his view.

The consequences of speech acts abound in this story. Paul's drunken sloganising destroys his life; the manager believes that his subversive speech makes him worse than even a violent criminal. We can detect the narrator's guilt about his meek agreement with this absurdity in the indirect speech with which it is reported. He may have been bullied into submission, but he submits — as he does to B.O.S. in other ways (he has swallowed B.O.S. products despite not liking them). His early insistence that he is "not gullible", if true, only underlines his moral cowardice. With his failure to stand up to the B.O.S. manager, he represents us all.[5]

Terror: Vladimir's view

Verloc certainly understands the link between materialism and perceptions of terror.

He surveyed through the park railings the evidences of the town's opulence and luxury with an approving eye. All these people had to be protected. Protection is the first necessity of opulence and luxury. They had to be protected; and their horses, carriages, houses, servants had to be protected; and the source of their wealth had to be protected in the heart of the city and the

[5]   Anthony Fothergill, 'Connoisseurs of terror and the political aesthetics of anarchism: *Nostromo* and *A Set of Six*', in Carola M. Kaplan, Peter Lancelot Mallios & Andrea White (eds.), *Conrad in the Twenty-First Century: Contemporary Approaches and Perspectives*, New York: Routledge, 2005, 137-154, at 145-147.

heart of the country; the whole social order favourable to their hygienic idleness had to be protected against the shallow enviousness of unhygienic labour.

This is a pleasingly complacent thought — Verloc, as a triple agent, is part of the protective effort twice over, and therefore onto a good thing. The irony, of course, is that Verloc does very little, and has no particular effect on events. But so keen is society to be protected that Verloc's contribution is never evaluated. In the same way, in today's fearful world, intelligence agencies struggle to keep effective surveillance, never mind control, of ideologically-driven terror; but increased funding follows failure, not success. Their job is almost impossible, but their incentives are highly skewed. However, Verloc is being found out. He is summoned to see Privy Councillor Wurmt, Chancelier d'Ambassade, who is "not very satisfied with the attitude of the police here". In the late 19th century, Britain, with its relatively tolerant laws and lack of means to keep tabs on people, was seen as a 'safe haven' for the anarchist terrorists who had bombed and shot their way through the crowned heads of Europe — rather as, until recently, Britain had been called, dismissively, Londonistan, for its tolerance of fanatical Muslim preachers spreading dissent and hate back to the Middle East from which they had been exiled.[6] Wurmt explains what is needed.

> 'What is desired,' said the man of papers, 'is the occurrence of something definite which should stimulate their vigilance. ... The vigilance of the police — and the severity of the magistrates. The general leniency of the judicial procedure here, and the utter absence of all repressive measures, are a scandal to Europe. What is wished for just now is the accentuation of the unrest — of the fermentation which undoubtedly exists — '

The First Secretary, Mr Vladimir, gives the ideological justification. Verloc is a Vice-President of a society called The Future of the Proletariat ("not anarchist in principle, but open to all shades of revolutionary opinion"), but Vladimir thinks Verloc "ought to be ashamed" of himself. "Isn't your society capable of anything else but printing this prophetic bosh in blunt type on this filthy paper — eh?" He wants the fight against political crime to regain some impetus, exploiting the middle classes' love of liberty.

[6]   Cf. Melanie Phillips, *Londonistan: How Britain is Creating a Terror State Within* (Updated edition), London: Gibson Square, 2007. The crackdown in London happened shortly after September 11th, 2001: 'Farewell, Londonistan?' *The Economist*, 31st Jan, 2002.

The imbecile bourgeoisie of this country make themselves the
accomplices of the very people whose aim is to drive them out of
their houses to starve in ditches. And they have the political power
still, if they only had the sense to use it for their preservation.

"What they want just now," opines Vladimir, "is a jolly good scare."
But the scare must be more than the minor thrill of a news bulletin.
The attack must be in Britain, as anything 'abroad' would not excite
people. And the attack (see Chapter Eight) should be against the
"fetish of to-day", science. It has to be irrational, unexplainable.

Much of *The Secret Agent* can be seen as a broadside against the
popular press, its simplifications and sensationalism, and the jaded
public that reads it. Vladimir gives vent to his frustration: he wants
to provoke outrage, but cannot.

An attempt upon a crowned head or on a president is sensational
enough in a way, but not so much as it used to be. It has entered
into the general conception of the existence of all chiefs of state.
It's almost conventional—especially since so many presidents
have been assassinated. Now let us take an outrage upon—say a
church. Horrible enough at first sight, no doubt, and yet not so
effective as a person of an ordinary mind might think. No matter
how revolutionary and anarchist in inception, there would be
fools enough to give such an outrage the character of a religious
manifestation. And that would detract from the especial alarm-
ing significance we wish to give to the act. A murderous attempt
on a restaurant or a theatre would suffer in the same way from
the suggestion of non-political passion: the exasperation of a
hungry man, an act of social revenge. All this is used up; it is no
longer instructive as an object lesson in revolutionary anarchism.
Every newspaper has ready-made phrases to explain such mani-
festations away. ... The sensibilities of the class you are attacking
are soon blunted. Property seems to them an indestructible
thing. You can't count on their emotions of pity or fear for very
long. A bomb outrage to have any influence on public opinion
now must go beyond the intention of vengeance or terrorism. It
must be purely destructive. It must be that, and only that, beyond
the faintest suspicion of any other object.

As we have seen, Vladimir's suggestion—order—is that Verloc
attack astronomy. "I defy the ingenuity of journalists to persuade the
public that any given member of the proletariat can have a personal
grievance against astronomy." "Yes ... the blowing up of the first
meridian is bound to raise a howl of execration."

Of course the terrorism of al-Qaeda and imitative attempts from
radical Islamists is not so pure. Would-be bomber Omar Khyam
mused about poisoning London's water supply (a "weak idea"), and

planned to blow up the Ministry of Sound nightclub, an attack on the "slags" dancing there.[7] Nevertheless he had an eye for the aesthetics of terror—a plan for coordinated attacks on London's gas supply was a "beautiful plan". The September 11th attack was a spectacular media event, with a powerful aesthetic behind it, as has been pointed many times.[8] The real-life murderers have clearly, like Mr Vladimir, been wrestling with the issue of the bourgeoisie's "jaded sensibilities." A common strategy is to attack transport, to threaten people in transit, symbols of global communication who furthermore have temporarily ceded control of their security to a piece of complex technology. It is not, perhaps, a bomb hurled into pure mathematics, but like Vladmir's plan, it defies the materialist logic of envy or even ideological or racial hatred. Muslims are the victims of most indiscriminate attacks by neo-fundamentalist Muslim terrorists.

One cannot and should not retreat in the face of threats of this nature (which is not to say that the West should not change its flawed policy in the Middle East, only that it should do so, if it does, for good reasons and not bad ones). But Conrad's analysis, seen through Vladimir's warped vision, accuses society of allowing its sensibilities to be jaded, and its threat perception to be moulded by sensational tales. Suicide bombers generally speaking target democracies, and the incidence of suicide bombing is not strongly correlated with the harshness of the regime against which the bomber is fighting.[9] As Conrad suggested, the key to understanding terror is the nature of the society within which it flourishes, not the 'external' forces that it suits governments to postulate. It is an enemy within, not without.

The Professor

Not all the anarchists are shams. The final member of Verloc's group is a physically unprepossessing individual known only as the Professor, and, as Conrad described him to Cunninghame Graham in 1907, "as regards the Professor I did not intend to make him despicable. He is incorruptible at any rate. In making him say 'madness and despair — give me that for a lever and I will move the world' I wanted to give him a note of perfect sincerity. At the worst he is a megalomaniac of an extreme type. And every extremist is respectable."

[7]   'Waiting for al-Qaeda's next bomb', *The Economist,* 3rd May, 2007.
[8]   Gray, *Al Qaeda and What it Means to be Modern.*
[9]   Robert A. Pape, *Dying to Win: The Strategic Logic of Suicide Terrorism,* New York: Random House, 2005.

The Professor is an absolute radical, a man without pity, a former chemist who is in love with bombs (he makes the bomb that kills Stevie). He is a total nihilist, to the point of his carrying around a bomb of his own devising, with a detonator in his pocket, on which he always keeps his hand. Once he presses it, there are twenty seconds before the bomb goes off. This arrangement has two advantages. First, it keeps the police from him. "To deal with a man like me," he boasts to Ossipon, "you require sheer, naked, inglorious heroism." And second, the delay to the bomb allows a moment of exultation in the joy of the nihilistic enterprise.

> 'Phew!' whistled Ossipon, completely appalled. 'Twenty seconds! Horrors! You mean to say that you could face that? I should go crazy—'

> 'Wouldn't matter if you did. Of course, it's the weak point of this special system, which is only for my own use. The worst is that the manner of exploding is always the weak point with us. I am trying to invent a detonator that would adjust itself to all conditions of action, and even to unexpected changes of conditions. A variable and yet perfectly precise mechanism. A really intelligent detonator.'

No doubt such detonators have now been developed.

The Professor stands aside from social conventions, he defines himself independently. It is his personality that counts over and above all other things. The mere profession of evil intent is not enough: the Professor needs technology and personality, and needs to engender a particular perception of himself.

> 'I have the means to make myself deadly, but that by itself, you understand, is absolutely nothing in the way of protection. What is effective is the belief those people have in my will to use the means. That's their impression. It is absolute. Therefore I am deadly.'

> 'There are individuals of character amongst that lot too,' muttered Ossipon ominously.

> 'Possibly. But it is a matter of degree obviously, since, for instance, I am not impressed by them. Therefore they are inferior. They cannot be otherwise. Their character is built upon conventional morality. It leans on the social order. Mine stands free from everything artificial. They are bound in all sorts of conventions. They depend on life, which, in this connection, is a historical fact surrounded by all sorts of restraints and considerations, a complex organised fact open to attack at every point; whereas I

depend on death, which knows no restraint and cannot be attacked. My superiority is evident.'

In the previous chapter we discussed too deep a faith in fact. Here, the Professor is trying to escape the power of fact altogether. Inferior people are bound by facts; he wants to get away from any kind of restraint. Ultimately, even the revolutionaries are similarly bound by social convention, because they want to revolutionise. He is not interested in change so much as destruction; creation can look after itself.

> To break up the superstition and worship of legality should be our aim. Nothing would please me more than to see Inspector Heat and his likes take to shooting us down in broad daylight with the approval of the public. Half our battle would be won then; the disintegration of the old morality would have set in in its very temple. That is what you ought to aim at. But you revolutionists will never understand that. You plan the future, you lose yourselves in reveries of economical systems derived from what is; whereas what's wanted is a clean sweep and a clear start for a new conception of life. That sort of future will take care of itself if you will only make room for it. Therefore I would shovel my stuff in heaps at the corners of the streets if I had enough for that; and as I haven't, I do my best by perfecting a really dependable detonator.

Who needs Guantánamo more, the United States or al-Qaeda? There is an unholy alliance, unstated and perhaps unconscious, implicit in those words of the Professor's, for they describe both Mr Vladimir's view of the situation—he is frustrated by the legal impediments to the surveillance and incarceration of the anarchists—and that of Chief Inspector Heat—who has a deeply instrumental view of catching criminals and would like clearer and more understandable 'rules of engagement.' *The Secret Agent* is often taken to be a pessimistic book about British society, which it certainly is, but there is a positive message to be taken away from it. With its tolerance of outsiders and restraint of legal officers, the British system, which has grown up over a thousand years of continuous history, planned by no-one, adapting to circumstances, does at least prevent the Professors, the Vladimirs and the Heats from getting their way.

The Professor is the *ne plus ultra* of scepticism; he repudiates facts, he repudiates social structures. The result is horrific. The "inferior" people about whose deaths he fantasises are bound by historical fact, the "restraints and conventions" of "social order". We have already seen that Conrad fully accepts that these conventions cannot be grounded in any deep foundational way, but that he is not at all sceptical of their value. Being bound by convention, allowing one-self to be restrained — these are basic human traits that make complex society possible.[10]

There is, of course, nothing that can be done about total nihilists like the Professor or Osama bin Laden. Argument cannot suffice; there is nothing reasonable there to engage. Although there has been much clodhopping about the Middle East by the USA and its allies to provoke him, bin Laden also professes outrage about the *reconquista* in Spain that was completed in 1492. It is not very clear what can be done about that. Conrad's main hope is that nihilists will be hoist on their own petard; in the story 'The informer' (written immediately before *The Secret Agent*), in which the Professor plays a walk-on part, we are told that "He perished a couple of years afterwards in a secret laboratory through the premature explosion of one of his improved detonators." But Conrad is very clear that if the authorities suspend, however temporarily, their moral principles in the interests of security, then the nihilists' work is being done for them.

We began our survey of Conrad's political work and ideas with a discussion of imperialism, which brought us Kurtz, and ended with nihilism, which furnished us with the Professor. How close they are; both products of frustration with restraint, of the belief that people (super-people, *Übermenschen*) are denied their true creativity and destiny by the historical accident of social conditioning. They each free themselves from that constraint, Kurtz by going into the African jungle, the Professor by retreating into himself and working "alone, quite alone, absolutely alone".

There is a crucial difference between them. The Professor remains within European society, and as such becomes an oppositional, destructive figure. Kurtz, with the power of the Company behind him, is in power and has total control over his environment. These are different contexts, and the two behave differently yet consistently. The Professor flourishes where protection is the supreme value; the source of Kurtz's power, however, is the desire of his company, and his civilisation, to export its values and to suppress "savage customs".

The parallels with today's political world seem too strong to ignore. The Western democracies are highly functional societies conferring many benefits on those that live there; one important

[10] Paul Seabright, *The Company of Strangers: A Natural History of Economic Life*, Princeton: Princeton University Press, 2004.

piece of evidence for this is the number of people who desire to move into them (and are prepared pay enormous sums of money to do so), compared to the trickle leaving. But in a world where 'homeland security' and 'exporting democracy' are two of the biggest watchwords, democracy is being squeezed between the Professor and Kurtz, by their unwitting collaborators, Mr Vladimir and the Company. When the means of protection, and the means of exporting its values, undermine the moral basis for a society, another direction is needed.

Chapter Ten

Joseph Conrad Today: Practical Unreason

We have followed, through the course of our investigation, the political thinking of Joseph Conrad, beginning with his critique of the unsupportable self-confidence underpinning imperialism and globalisation. It is not feasible to create the sort of deep affirmation of society that is required. Failure to do so spawns the guilt and pity that accompany the perception of diversion from one's ideals, which lay a foundation for a type of revolutionary activity. But this too is flawed. For Conrad, character is uncertain, to counter the darkness within our hearts (individual and collective), we need a practical ethic of work, duty and fidelity. Even these, however, have no foundational basis, and cannot be proved superior by science; conversely, science, though a genuine source of important knowledge, is not self- supporting either. But too great a desire for, or reliance on, foundational projects will result, for those who are sufficiently clear-headed (a Nietzsche or Rimbaud figure), in a destructive nihilism which its most notorious practitioner dubbed "The horror!" with his final breath.

Though Conrad was not systematic, he was political. And his politics were, generally-speaking, small-c conservative, using the term as I have defined it elsewhere, as a general principle of caution, tolerance and humility in the face of enormous epistemological disadvantage.[1] He did not comment on mainstream politics often, but there is some thinly-veiled commentary in a novel co-written with Ford Madox Ford, *The Inheritors*, where two Tory politicians are caricatured. Balfour (from the conservative wing of the Conserva-

[1]   Kieron O'Hara, *After Blair: David Cameron and the Conservative Tradition*, Cambridge: Icon Books, 2007.

tive Party[2]) is given a positive characterisation (as a character confusingly named Churchill), while the Liberal Unionist Chamberlain, not a small-c conservative at all,[3] becomes the sinister Gurnard. Even though the novel is more Ford than Conrad, the latter at least allowed it out under his name.

Conrad's conservatism causes problems for those who recognise Conrad's genius, but who are implacably opposed to right wing politics. The distinguished critic J. Hillis Miller writes about previous scholarship condemning Conrad for being any one of a number of distasteful things, including a racist, an imperialist, a paralysed sceptical ironist, a sexist — but is equally horrified that he might be a political conservative who despises the class struggle.[4] Even though one can be criticised for the first few items on the list, can one properly be condemned for being a *conservative*? Isn't that kind of OK? Surely even a non-conservative must think it is acceptable to be a conservative, unacceptable to be racist?

Ultimately, Conrad has an ideal (expressed perhaps most clearly in *The Nigger of the "Narcissus"*, 'Typhoon' and *The Mirror of the Sea*) of the crew of a ship, getting through the merciless, immense, uncomprehending ocean, against the odds through their skill, their interrelationships, and a sailing vessel which respects the sea. The mercantile marine is a place to be tested, where the value of duty, fidelity and system are clearly revealed, and where useless hierarchies and free riders are exposed as such.

On the other hand, his pessimism is thoroughgoing. The mercantile marine provides a model for society, but unlike most ideologues, he sees no way of getting everyone to agree on that model, or of forcing the model into place. Unlike Fukuyama, he cannot see inevitability in the acceptance of his "simple principles"; unlike Chomsky, he does not think that people are prevented by evil forces and capitalistic structures from seeing their own interests properly; unlike George Bush and the neo-conservative thinkers of the Washington Beltway he does not think that the best principles can be imposed from without. *Nostromo* details an eminently rational attempt to reform a country that is doomed to fail. The outcome of the Company's rule in 'Heart of darkness' is Kurtz, and Conrad

[2]   O'Hara, *After Blair*, 104-107.
[3]   O'Hara, *After Blair*, 107-111.
[4]   J. Hillis Miller, 'Foreword', in Carola M. Kaplan, Peter Lancelot Mallios & Andrea White (eds.), *Conrad in the Twenty-First Century*, New York: Routledge, 2005, 1-14, at 4.

holds out no hope for anything better. V.S. Naipaul's *A Bend in the River* extends the argument with the thought that the particular refinement of European imperialism is the ultimately irrelevant 'idea' behind it, and contextualises the European rape of Africa as one of a long list of such barbarous enterprises, including those perpetrated by African tribes and post-independence African leaders. When the Malays of Sambir end Lingard's monopoly of trade in *An Outcast of the Islands*, they are no better off.

So how does this make Conrad relevant today? In the first place, he is very sceptical about anyone's ability to understand the world enough to make far-reaching plans, or sufficiently to understand people (individuals, communities or nations) to be able, legitimately, to decide where their interests lie. Revolutions, or schemes to organise society on the basis of scientific or technical lines, are doomed to fail, and, when imposed by force, however well-meaning, inherently criminal.

Secondly, he was extremely suspicious of the idea of progress. Inside people, or civilisations, he discerned a heart of darkness, and impressive technological or political developments merely make that darkness easier to express. That is not an argument against material progress, but rather that such progress will not solve our problems, and may make (some aspects of) them worse. The World Wide Web is a fine thing, one of the greatest pieces of communication technology the world has seen. Its benefits are enormous.[5] But we cannot ignore the downsides. It trivialises some debates. It can be used as a communication tool by unsavoury individuals and organisations. It reinforces the liberal ideological hegemony. Although it empowers some of the powerless, we should not forget that keeping some people powerless is a good thing. We cannot resolve these debates without respecting the continuity of political science; society has not changed to such an extent that the insights of Plato, Machiavelli, Locke, Burke, Smith, Marx, Oakeshott and Rawls can be discarded.[6]

[5]   About which I have written elsewhere. Tim Berners-Lee, Wendy Hall, James A. Hendler, Kieron O'Hara, Nigel Shadbolt & Daniel J. Weitzner, 'A framework for Web Science', *Foundations and Trends in Web Science*, 1(1), 2006, 1-134.

[6]   Kieron O'Hara & David Stevens, *inequality.com: Power, Politics and the Digital Divide*, Oxford: Oneworld, 2006. That is not to say that the theories of any or all of these luminaries are being recommended in this book; they are not. But they all repay reading, even in the digital age.

A related idea is that history has a direction, which crops up all over Western thought.[7] Ultimately, it is a Christian idea, exploited most notoriously by Hegel, and through him, Marx, and most recently Fukuyama. This is surely nonsense, shown to be so by the best refuters of historical theories, events. Conrad sets out the accidents that get in the way, and the incorrigibility of those who resist progress, or who use it for their own decidedly unprogressive ends, very clearly indeed.

Conrad's work also dramatises the complete inability of theories and plans to determine the future, a failing of both right and left. So free markets will handle the distribution of resources most fairly and efficiently, will they? An equal society can be created by taking wealth from the rich and giving to the poor, can it? Our gender or class identities are more important than the delicate societies, hierarchies and coalitions of opposites which form organically, do we? Yeah, right. Abstractions don't work. In all his fiction, Conrad provides us with a strong sense of place, time and context. He resists overarching ideas, and shows us how it is impossible to imagine that there can be one solution for the problems of Sambir, London, Costaguana, Russia, the poop-deck of the *Patna*, the forecastle of the *Narcissus*, Toulon or the Company's Inner Station.

Many of our problems are basically insoluble. There is an ill-tempered debate between those who think that we have to adjust our behaviour to prevent climate change, and those who think we have to adapt as it happens. Actually, there is no 'solution': we will have to do both, because the effects of the pollution we have created over the last couple of centuries will take centuries to go away, even if we changed radically now. We have a growing population worldwide, which we are likely to continue to be able to feed. But many people scrabbling over land and resources (especially water) will not be easy to manage. Ethnic hatred, religious bigotry, ruthless profiteering, organised crime, not to mention the decadence of those in the most 'advanced' democracies, are problems that will remain with us for decades. To 'deal' with them will require hard work, not brilliant Utopian schemes or hard-edged warfare.

Conrad had very little faith in reason to solve our problems. This, perhaps, is one explanation of his continued relevance today. With simple moral principles, chiefly fidelity and loyalty, a focus on work

[7]   John Gray, *Enlightenment's Wake: Politics and Culture at the Close of the Modern Age*, London: Routledge, 1995, and *Heresies: Against Progress and Other Illusions*, London: Granta, 2004.

and community, and eschewing the search for moral foundations, we can get along, for a limited period, within limited parameters. We know we can, because we do. But so many political thinkers ignore that basic fact, and prefer to focus on how we *might* get along, in *different* circumstances, with *different* economic relations and *different* personalities that do not as a matter of fact obtain. Conrad reminds us of what we know works, and restates what ought to be truisms (but aren't) with clarity, while casting his impeccably jaundiced eye over our visionary aspirations. On 3rd December, 2007, the 150th anniversary of Conrad's birth (shortly after the centenary of *The Secret Agent*), there is still no more important task to be performed.

Reading Conrad

Joseph Conrad's writing spanned a little over thirty years, only a moderate career in temporal terms, and his *oeuvre* is lengthy but manageable for the keen student. My own humble opinion is that six of his works are classics that repay multiple rereadings, with a place on the shelves of any discerning reader of literature. They are *The Nigger of the "Narcissus": A Tale of the Forecastle* (1897), 'Heart of darkness' (1899), *Lord Jim: A Tale* (1900), *Nostromo: A Tale of the Seaboard* (1904), *The Secret Agent: A Simple Tale* (1907) and *Under Western Eyes: A Novel* (1911).

As well as these, he completed eight further novels. His 'Malay Trilogy', consisting of *Almayer's Folly: A Story of an Eastern River* (1895), *An Outcast of the Islands* (1896) and *The Rescue: A Romance of the Shallows* (1920) should be the next port of call — the trilogy is written in reverse, with the events of *The Rescue* set about 1860, *An Outcast* around 1872, and *Almayer's Folly* in the 1880s. There is much of value in *Victory: An Island Tale* (1915), *The Shadow-Line: A Confession* (1917) and *The Rover* (1923). *Chance: A Tale in Two Parts* (1913) is flawed, while the main interest of *The Arrow of Gold: A Story Between Two Notes* (1919) is to provide some background for Conrad's period as a young man in Marseilles; it is the least of his novels. *Suspense: A Napoleonic Novel* (1925) was left incomplete at his death; the 80,000-word fragment was edited for publication by Richard Curle, but holds little interest for the casual reader.

Although primarily a novelist, he was an accomplished writer of short fiction, and produced seven collections. The two that stand out are *Youth, a Narrative: And Two Other Stories* (1902), which contains not only 'Heart of darkness' but also 'Youth' and 'The end of the tether', and *Typhoon: And Other Stories* (1903), in which can be found 'Typhoon', 'Amy Foster', 'Falk' and 'Tomorrow'. *Tales of Unrest* (1898) contains 'Karain: a memory', 'An outpost of progress' and 'The lagoon'. *A Set of Six* (1908) contains 'The informer: an ironic tale' and 'An anarchist: a desperate tale'. *'Twixt Land and Sea: Three Tales* (1912) contains 'The secret sharer'. *Within the Tides: Tales* (1915) is perhaps the least distinguished of his volumes of short fiction. *Tales of Hearsay* (1925, edited by Richard Curle with R.B. Cunninghame Graham) contains 'Prince Roman' and 'The tale'. The four works narrated by Marlow are 'Youth', 'Heart of darkness', *Lord Jim* and *Chance*.

He produced four works of non-fiction created from magazine articles. *The Mirror of the Sea: Memories and Impressions* (1906) is, in my view, the best of his non-fiction (currently an unfashionable opinion, though also Conrad's own), containing a number of more or less profound, more or less over-written essays about his sea-going days. *A Personal Record: Some Reminiscences* (1912) is the nearest Conrad ever got to a memoir, and therefore clearly of interest to the Conradian. It was developed out of a series of articles he wrote for Ford Madox Ford's *English Review* in 1908-9. *Notes on Life and Letters* (1921) and *Last Essays* (1926, edited by Curle) bring together most of the rest of his important essays. All of the individual essays mentioned in this book are in *Notes*, with the exception of 'Geography and some explorers', which appeared in *Last Essays*.

In addition to these, Conrad wrote 'Author's notes' for many of his books, most of which were composed between 1917 and 1920 for a collected edition of his works. These notes are generally slight, but usually of interest, even if they are often designed to conceal rather than reveal their sources. The 'Notes' to *The Nigger of the "Narcissus"* (written in 1897), *A Personal Record* (also including 'A familiar preface', written in 1911) and *Under Western Eyes* are the most important. Conrad's letters have been edited by a team including Lawrence Davies, Frederick R. Karl, Owen Knowles, Gene M. Moore and J.H. Stape, and published by Cambridge University Press; the ninth and final volume is scheduled to appear to coincide with the Conrad anniversary. The final significant writings of Conrad were his 'Congo diaries', written during his African trip of 1890. These are two notebooks, the first of which is reproduced in *Last Essays*; the other, sometimes called 'The up-river book', appears in the Norton Critical Edition of 'Heart of darkness'.

On Conrad's life, Jocelyn Baines, *Joseph Conrad: A Critical Biography*, Harmondsworth: Pelican, 1971, is the most straightforwardly factual account. Frederick R. Karl, *Joseph Conrad: The Three Lives*, London: Faber and Faber, 1979 is rather more ambitious. See also John Batchelor, *The Life of Joseph Conrad: A Critical Biography*, Oxford:

Blackwell, 1994, and Zdzislaw Najder, *Joseph Conrad: A Chronicle*, Cambridge: Cambridge University Press, 1983, re-issued in 2007, among many others; Najder is the prime English-language source for the Polish years. For reference there is Owen Knowles, *A Conrad Chronology*, London: Macmillan, 1989, and for an easily digestible chapter, Owen Knowles, 'Conrad's life', in J.H. Stape, *The Cambridge Companion to Joseph Conrad*, Cambridge: Cambridge University Press, 1996, 1-24.

Stape's *Companion* is one of many good volumes of introductory, yet perceptive, essays on Conrad's work, while a reliable dictionary-type companion is Owen Knowles and Gene M. Moore (eds.), *Oxford Reader's Companion to Conrad*, Oxford: Oxford University Press, 2000. *Conradiana* is an academic journal devoted to matters Conradian.

Index

Index

Pinter, Harold 86
Plato 94, 121
Poland 1, 4, 10, 12, 13, 26, 48-50, 79-81,
    95n, 102
'Poland revisited' 79
Poradowska, Marguerite 6-7
Prescott, John 57
'Prince Roman' 48, 50, 54, 79, 80
Putin, Vladimir 49

Rawls, John 53, 121
Rescue, The 8, 10
Rice, Condoleezza 16
Richardson, Brian 70, 71-72
Rimbaud, Arthur 119
Rom, Léon 21
Rousseau, Jean-Jacques 78
Rover, The 1, 10-11, 83-85, 101
Russell, Bertrand 10
Russia 1, 4, 13, 26, 35, 40, 48-50, 51, 80,
    81-83, 102

Saddam Hussein 54, 60
Said, Edward 30, 31, 35
Salisbury, Marquess of 15, 52
Sanguszko, Prince Roman 80
Secret Agent, The 1, 2, 9, 12, 13, 19,
    35-36, 44, 54, 56, 69, 81, 89-90,
    105-110, 111-118, 123
    Adolf Verloc 98, 105-106, 107,
        108-110, 111-113
    Chief Inspector Heat 109-110, 116
    Michaelis 56, 107-110
    Mr Vladimir 106, 107, 108, 110,
        112-114, 116, 118
    Ossipon 92, 108-109, 115
    Stevie 44-45, 54, 105, 106, 108, 110,
        115
    The Professor 107, 114-118
    Winnie Verloc 54, 98, 105-106, 109,
        110
    Yundt 108-109
'Secret sharer, The' 9, 62, 64-65
Shadow-Line, The 10, 11, 28, 54, 69-70,
    72, 73, 89
Shakespeare, William 69, 71
Singer, Peter 53
Singh, Frances B. 25, 30
Smith, Adam 121
Soviet Union, The, see 'Russia'
Spencer, Herbert 96
Spenser, Edmund 84
Stacpoole, Henry de Vere 76
Stalin, Josef 48, 58
Suspense 11

Switzerland 7, 57

'Tale, The' 93
Thatcher, Margaret 57, 92
Third Man, The 57
Tobias, Randall 16
Tolstoy, Leo 1, 59, 60
Tourneur, Maurice 10
Tsvangirai, Morgan 46
'Typhoon' 15, 76-77, 120

Umberto I 51
Under Western Eyes 9, 12, 13, 24, 30n,
    39, 40-42, 45, 48, 50, 56-57, 58, 61,
    81-83, 88, 102, 107
    Razumov 24, 39, 40-42, 61, 62, 64,
        70, 81-83, 88, 98, 100
United Kingdom, see 'England'
United States of America 3, 10, 116,
    117

Venezuela 2, and see 'Hugo Chávez'
Victory 10, 28, 36, 43, 44, 61, 65-66, 84,
    85, 88, 92, 95, 98, 101, 102-103
Victory (film) 10

Warnock, Mary 57
Watt, Ian 88, 89n, 96n, 97, 101n
Watts, Cedric 101
'"Well done"' 28, 68, 74
Wells, H.G. 2, 8, 52
Williams, Bernard 64
Wilson, Woodrow 95
Wittgenstein, Ludwig 99
Wolfowitz, Paul 16
Woolf, Virginia 11

Young, Francis Brett 76
'Youth' 69

Zhuwarara, Rino 30
Zimbabwe 45-46